WELL DONE!

WELL DONE!

Ken Adams

Piccadilly • London

Phototypeset from author's disk by Piccadilly Press.
Printed and bound by Progressive Printing Limited, Essex
for the publishers Piccadilly Press Ltd.,
5 Castle Road, London NW1 8PR

A catalogue record for this book is available from the
British Library

ISBN: 1 85340 347 4

Ken Adams lives in Greater Manchester. He teaches a great
variety of subjects to children, and adults, of all ages and
abilities. He has taught all his own children and one of his
sons passed "A" level maths at the age of 9. He has written a
number of books including the bestsellers, YOUR CHILD CAN
BE A GENIUS, STRAIGHT "A"s AT GCSE, and YOUR CHILD CAN BE
TOP OF THE CLASS. He has also written the *Samson Superslug*
books which have been serialised on television. This is his first
book for Piccadilly Press.

CONTENTS

Introduction

WORKING WITH FAMILIES AND CHILDREN

"So you write books, do you?" said the taxi driver.

I nodded, hoping that he was skilled enough to manoeuvre through traffic at this frantic speed, as well as look across at me.

"Perhaps you could teach my kids English and maths," he continued, raising a quizzical eyebrow. "And my daughter is hopeless at science."

I nodded again.

"I'll come on Friday," I muttered, as we rocketed along the High Street, and prayed that I would live to see the day.

On Friday, he showed me up to a comfortably furnished room above a car-spares shop, then disappeared while I laid out my educational paraphernalia. When he re-appeared, he led a troop of children across the threshold and into the room, headed by a bemused-looking five-year-old, each subsequent child slightly bigger than the last. There were ten in all.

"There's my lot, my brother's, my sister's, and my cousin's two. Okay?" he said, cheerfully. Twenty quizzical brown eyes looked up at me.

"Fine, fine," I said, trying to make light of the matter.

"Any more?"

"We-ell, since you ask," he said, stroking his chin thoughtfully, "there are a couple of four-year-olds, a three-year-old, and three babies. Perhaps you can turn them into geniuses or something."

I settled for the ten, and the two hour lesson was solved using graded work sheets.

ONE-TO-ONE

Usually, though, a tutoring group is just the one pupil or maybe two. This is virtually essential when teaching a remedial child to read, or, in any case, when seeking to fulfil the potential of anyone.

Going from school teaching in the day-time, to tutoring in a family home in the evening was a breath of fresh air in many respects. In school, apart from having to cope with thirty or so highly individualistic minds, a teacher is obliged to toe the line to the ethos of school and education authority. Normally, one at least gave lip service to current education philosophy, but throughout training and in the classroom nobody seemed to give too much attention to how children actually learn. For me, if that question was solved, teaching would become immeasurably easier. Working with children in their own homes lifted the constraints of classroom organisation and directives from above, and freed me to find out how to overcome children's learning difficulties.

CHILD GENIUS

My son became the first real subject for extended "study", although that was not my intention from the outset. One day, I found that my ten-month-old baby son could read words from an A-B-C book, even when the pictures were covered. Subsequently, as a toddler, he developed symptoms akin to mental frustration, scrambling endlessly backwards and forwards across the furniture in the front room, rather like a caged tiger. My solution to his behavioural problem was to extend his reading and teach him to count. Immediately, he became focused, calm and content (psychologists would argue that he was seeking attention, but he'd had plenty of that before): John developed at a fantastic pace, as I spent hours planning staged learning periods of just fifteen minutes per day.

In case I "missed something" of crucial importance to intellectual development, I widened the spread of activities to include, beside maths and English, investigations, puzzles, problem solving, games (draughts, chess), piano playing, and creative activities. Everything was soaked up by the small child's sponge of a mind. Eventually, when he was nine, he reached university entrance standard in maths, in between organising triple jump competitions with his brothers up and down the corridor. His younger brothers followed a similar path, though not quite so dramatic, reading as toddlers, yet buzzing with feverish enthusiasm for every boyish activity under the sun.

TUTORING IN FAMILIES

After ten years of helping my sons, I graduated to tutoring other children in their family homes. They have come from every possible background and ethnic mix: English, Asian, Afro-Caribbean, Chinese; children in terraced houses, caravans, a mansion with its own lake; some were physically disabled, mentally disabled, rapier fast learners, or average. Most, though, have been a joy to work with, eager to learn in the main, and, without exception, possessing a perceptive and outrageous sense of humour. Not one has been unteachable, especially when state-of-the-art learning methods have been used to overcome particular difficulties.

The parents have been teachers, doctors, solicitors, directors of large firms, factory workers, shop workers, shop owners, the unemployed...a mosaic across all class divides. What has struck me in every learning situation, is how similar is the basic learning process of these children. Fatima, an astoundingly talented five-year-old, employs the same thinking processes as my "A" level maths and science students; and Wei, who has just come from mainland China, and is learning English and maths with me, could be any one of hundreds that I have taught before. The only difference has been that one child may *know* more than, or differently to, another; and one child may learn faster than another.

PARENTS AND CHILDREN

Parents are best placed to find out what their child knows. I usually leave some work sheets with them, they try them out, and report back after a week. They often have pre-conceived notions that "he is not clever" or "that one can't do maths". They can have a simplistic idea of how children should be educated based around reading, writing and arithmetic, and are incensed if these are taught badly at school, quite understandably. One eight-year-old, an Indian Moslem boy, had been taught all his tables up to twenty times, his father mistakenly believing that this would guarantee success in the educational system. His progress in other areas was hardly average, and I had great difficulty persuading the father that we needed to concentrate elsewhere, and drop the tables for a while.   Sometimes a tutoring situation has been very imperfect. In one family, the parents expected me to teach university entrance to an eighteen-year-old in chemistry, biology and maths, and at the same time help a thirteen-year-old boy, and a slow learner of eight. In a one hour session each week, the older girl needed all my attention, as did each of the others. Part of their trouble was financial, the parents wanting to give equal help to all three whilst being able to afford too little tutoring help. Happily, now, the older girl is at university, and there is more time for the other two.

REMEDIAL PUPILS

The progress of some remedial children can be quite startling with individual help, if effective visualisation methods are employed (see later chapters).

Alison was in a school for remedial pupils, and improved so much in three months, that she was moved to the lower sets in a normal school. In the next six months she was moved up again, and over the following twelve months continued to improve, but more steadily (all this on one hour a week tutoring).

Eventually, her mother lost patience: "My friend's girl does much harder work than Alison," she said, and blamed her daughter (who was a real tryer) for being lazy.

I suppose, though, that the mother was reacting to the stigma of having a slow learning child. She should have shown more compassion; like the mother of a boy I teach whose sickness over many years has left him, at fifteen, with fore-shortened limbs and an inability to walk. He is now just learning how to add up and take away. Or Anne, who suffers from a degeneration of the nervous system that will lead to an early death. No sense of stigma here, only devotion and compassion, as their children struggle against almost overwhelming odds.

There is strong incentive to succeed as a tutor: "My mum says that if I don't get better at school by the summer, you're for the chop," said Melanie, aged ten, quite matter-of-factly. Unfortunately, Melanie's inability to concentrate at school is partly due to lack of confidence through failure in subjects like maths. With her mother promising a substantial reward for good progress, and my filling in the gaps in Melanie's knowledge, I might just be able to beat the deadline but it's going to be a close call.

ADVANTAGES

There are very significant advantages to working with families and their children. There are generally few discipline problems, because even a child who is a wild animal at school will behave in view and earshot of a parent. Also, over a myriad of cups of tea and coffee, many a roast dinner and excellent curry, the families become friends (the way to the teacher's heart is through his stomach, I suppose). As several parents have said, "You're not the teacher far removed from us, you're like us – just ordinary." What seems to have sealed this opinion for one family was my turning up at the house on a bicycle (in the middle of a fitness fad). Sadia collapsed into gales of laughter when her mother asked me where my car was parked.

In his or her own home, a child is inevitably more relaxed than at school, and this relaxation transfers to the learning situation. I can ferret out the psychology behind failures more easily than I can at school, partly because the parents are always there to explain the background and personality of their child, and also any ongoing problems.

I can concentrate on the particular difficulties of each child I work with. I can view the child as a whole, knowing both how he or she performs academically, and also the home background.

Working with children and their families has taught me virtually all that I know about how children learn.

Chapter One

HOW CHILDREN FAIL

I was teaching Stephen, aged seven, about the four points of the compass – North, South, East and West – and posed this problem:

"If I stand facing North, then turn through half a circle, in which direction am I now facing?"

Stephen turned his face away and stared into space. You could hear a pin drop in the room.

"South," he said, finally.

I asked him exactly how he worked it out. "I was in the playground at school," he said, "in the netball circle. I looked at one end of the playground. That was North. Then I turned halfway round. I was facing the opposite way, which is South."

In doing this, Stephen, a clever boy, was following an effective problem solving sequence.

1. He focused (concentrated) on the problem and created a mind picture of it.

2. He then tried to match, or near-match, what he had in his memory (knowledge of N-S-E-W), and a "half-circle" turn, with the information. It is a complex process that requires effort and confidence, as well as certain knowledge: Stephen had to create and hold in his mind three

simultaneous mind-pictures – of my problem, of a half-turn, and of the points of the compass. To make this easier to do he transported the whole problem and its resolution into the school playground (another image or picture to create in the mind).

Apart from the concentrated mental effort required (and some children definitely lack the ability to concentrate this well), a child (like an adult) needs to create those mind images or pictures, and there must be closely related information in memory to link to. For example, if Stephen had no idea of the points of the compass, he would not be able to link that information with what was relayed through his sense organs (in this case eyes and ears). Without some close affinity of this sort, there would be no meaning, no match with anything in memory, and Stephen would fail.

LACK OF CONCENTRATION

1. BILU'S STORY
Clearly, focusing attention, or concentration, is vital – it *drives* information into memory. Bilu is a Hindu boy I have known since he was a toddler, and I have helped his older sisters for several years. Eighteen months ago, his school was about to dispatch him to a remedial unit because "he could not learn." His parents were angry, because they felt that the school had made no real effort with him. They disliked the open-plan form of schooling, and the laissez-faire attitude that pupils find their "own level". In Bilu's case this amounted to abandoning everything even remotely connected with maths, English, or science, and becoming, in effect, a giggling, chattering,

poking, prodding and disruptive nuisance. Bilu's parents' solution was to remove him from his school, and embark on a short-term, aggressive programme of parental tuition (a little too aggressive for my liking). What they did mirrored in some ways Antipodean experiments with remedial children, who are made to concentrate by slapping the table noisily in front of them when their attention wanders. They also employed one-to-one tuition.

Bilu is now ten, and from being hardly able to add three and five in his head, he now solves complicated area problems involving long multiplication without resource to paperwork, and writes long, interesting, well-spelt and well-punctuated essays. His parents had correctly identified, in part, the cause of his failure, although the means they employed to a reasonably satisfactory end seem to me to have a parallel in the trainer's whip. There is more than one way to train a tiger though. Rewards and incentives are usually encouragement enough to achieve focus.

Bilu's case is a common one. He is not a quick learner, and therefore needs learning material to be especially clearly presented, and staged carefully. Some children can abstract ideas and information from a learning situation that is not particularly well presented at one time. With a little prompting, they can visualise and understand what the teacher intends them to understand. Children like Bilu find this extremely difficult, and lose confidence when they see that others understand what they do not. This sets up a cycle of failure, loss of confidence, fear of failure and the learning situation. The child falls further and further behind, feeling that he can do nothing right, often getting sympathy only through exaggerating his inability to understand. The answer is to ensure good, structured learning, particularly at the beginning of school life. Identifying slower learners at this stage can ensure that learning material is appropriate to their needs.

2. BEN'S STORY

Some years ago a father called me in and begged for help with his son, who was nearly eight and could not read a single word. The school situation was similar to Bilu's. The school had explained that Ben "could not retain anything for any length of time." In the meantime, Ben was racing round his classroom and the corridors of the school having a whale of a time, and "expressing his personality" to its fullest. Since he was not static for long enough to have a single word placed in front of him, I did not find it surprising that he did not retain anything. After five minutes with him (his father's presence ensured that he sat down and was relatively still for that time), I could tell that he was a very smart boy, perfectly able to read.

"You will have to get him to concentrate," I told his father. So I came once a week for half-an-hour and used a reading scheme starter book, and his father continued daily in-between. There was little need for coercion. His father simply said, "Until you have done your half-an-hour, you don't go out to play or watch TV." Ben sat at a table in a quiet side-room so that there were few distractions. In three weeks, he could read quite well, and his father presented him with reading book to the headmaster, who proclaimed the whole thing "a miracle". Confidence restored, Ben was absolutely beside himself with joy. This tough little lad ran down his home street to show all his friends that he was "just like them now."

BEING TAUGHT THE WRONG WAY FOR THE CHILD

James also failed in his reading. At ten years of age, he is a motor-cycle fanatic, a grass-track racing champion for his area. When I go to tutor him he's always up to his arm-pits in motor-oil and motor-cycle parts in the adjoining garage. He knows *everything* about engines, but he stumbles over reading words. This is surprising, because I taught him to read as a four-year-old pre-schooler, and he certainly could read almost as well as he does now. Between then and now, his parents assigned me to teach his older brother Andrew, who goes to university this year to start an engineering course. Starting again with James, far from being top of the class, he is far behind, his confidence shaken over all aspects of school-work.

"Why, James?" I ask him. "You're a clever boy."

"I know," he says. "I was the best in the Infants."

Working with James now, I agree with his school who say that he "works hard" and seems to concentrate. However, like many remedial pupils, he needs new learning to be carefully staged, and laid out exceptionally clearly. He finds difficulty in learning spelling in lists, for example, but lay the words out in a "web" or "map" so that he can examine structure more carefully, and he learns as well as the next boy.

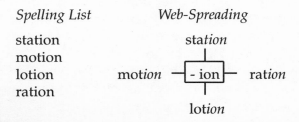

Spelling List

station
motion
lotion
ration

Web-Spreading

station

motion —|- ion |— ration

lotion

James fails because he has difficulty learning unless items and concepts are clearly separated. He is not a candidate who learns well by osmosis. In fact, everyone learns better and quicker if concepts (ideas) are isolated for learning, although most people abstract something meaningful from a confused scenario. Some people can do this much better than others, and psychologists have suggested that the ability to do so is a way of grading intelligence.

In James's case, I have to assess his level of attainment in all areas and, by careful staging and grading of work, build on what he knows. In the school system, this is not done effectively enough: there is a syllabus to follow, and the relentless pressure to move on to new work does not allow for "re-starting" a child at a lower level. If pre-requisite stages are not tackled, however, James will simply not learn well and progress will grind to a halt. The school system should serve the individual child; rather than forcing the child to fit into the system.

DISAGREEABLE ENVIRONMENT

1. LOW EXPECTATIONS

Failure can mean many things. A few months ago, I was privileged to witness an amazing "experiment". An unmarried mother, the daughter of a friend, brought her new-born baby to her parents' house every day, and watched as her teenage aunty leant over her and repeated, again and again: "Hello. Hello. Hello."

Each day she did this, and little bright-eyed Sarah stared at her, mimicking the poking out of the tongue: "La, la, lel, lel, lo, lo..." and practised her gurgles, until, four weeks after birth, she could produce the exact sing-song copy of her aunty's: "Hello."

Later, at ten weeks, she could also repeat, "Mummy."

Sarah has great potential. Her family have exceptionally keen sight and hearing, which suggests a high order of production of mental "images" from sensory input. This has some bearing on learning ability, although it is just a fraction of the total equation.

However, Sarah's situation does not bode well for her. The estate where she lives is a drug pusher's haven, her uncle is on heroin and her mother is a heavy drinker. There are not likely to be valuable learning experiences which will translate into great intellectual development, and academic success.

2. LACK OF PARENTAL INVOLVEMENT

This is not to say that the children of the rich will necessarily fare much better. I teach Denzil in his home, a sprawling detached house set in several acres, with a lake in the grounds. His parents are both doctors, a surgeon and a general practitioner, who own a considerable amount of property. Denzil's parents are extremely busy people, and certainly have little time to oversee his progress at school. However, they recognise that he does not learn quickly like their daughter, and that he has got behind in maths and English. Denzil is anxious to learn at home, though mainly to please his parents. As long as he likes his tutor, and work is targeted to fit in with what he knows, he progresses very quickly indeed. I do notice, though, that his parents have applied some pressure: "I've got a stone cottage," he says, "and I can go to Greece this year; but only if I get better at work."

7

3. EXCEPTIONS

The Asian community generally puts a lot of time, effort and money into education. It is second only to religion. From the start, Asians set about inculcating a sense of the worth of learning:

"Education is so important," says Sadia's mother, "that we will take food from the breakfast table to pay for it."

Sadia's father is unemployed, and the family never has a holiday, yet they will pay for extra tutoring, work books, anything to give their children a "good start". Sadia sees this, and has developed a very positive attitude towards learning. She and her sisters, though not exceptionally quick learners, are heading for a university education.

LACK OF INTEREST

A more recent cause of failure stems from a child's belief that everything he or she learns must be interesting.

So: "This is boring," says Barry. "Maths is boring." As maths is to many, because, quite frankly, there *are* more appealing things for children to do than a maths sum, whether it is set in a practical way, or not. Barry is mad about football, so in the summer holidays he spends every spare minute playing with his friends. He is talented, so perhaps he will become centre for England (goodness knows, we need the talent), but if he breaks his leg he may wish he had some qualifications. Like adults, children would like to sample certain things, and discard others – play with their toys, but not clear up afterwards. Basing learning on interests (e.g. Barry's love of football) inevitably leads to a watering-down of the curriculum, and, anyway, Barry wants to *play* football, not do sums about it.

"Teachers are supposed to make work not boring," says Rubina to her teachers. Rubina is smart. She has seen that she can do what she wants to (which is not very much) if she manipulates her teachers, to whom the accusation of being a "boring teacher" is synonymous with being a "bad teacher". So, Rubina, who is another potentially brilliant child, fails.

It is an attitude developed to an extreme by David who basically, again, is very quick thinking. His answer to everything has been, "Kids should have fun, not do work," as a young child and into his teens. Now, he has left school and spends nearly all his time on the street corner. He is confused. He wants a home, a family and a good job, and he is not having much fun.

OTHER CAUSES OF FAILURE

Other causes of failure can be found both in the home and in the school. David's mother has been consistent in insisting that childhood is a "fun time", not to be disturbed by imposed schoolwork. David, understandably, has taken this philosophy on board, arguing with his teachers about the value of academic work. His mother has spent a life-time at the school complaining that her son should not be "picked on".

In practice, children glean a sense of the worth of education in the main from their parents' attitudes. The responsibility of tailoring learning to the ability of a child, however, should fall on the school. This aspect of failure, by not structuring learning sufficiently for easy learning, falls squarely on the shoulders of the educational system. Because of failures in this area, parents have increasingly taken it upon themselves to help their children at home.

IN CONCLUSION

The seeds of failure are many. Central are faulty teaching methods, including trying to introduce new concepts which do not match closely enough with what a child *knows*; especially for some children who are more dependant on carefully staged mind-building and the use of concrete material and diagrams, etc, than others. There is often not enough repetition of tasks within a period of time to make recall instinctive. To understand is important, but it is not enough. As will be explained in the next chapter, recall of what you learn depends either on "pegging" (linking learning with something concrete in your child's mind), or meaningful repetition to the point where recall is instinctive.

Other causes of failure are lack of parental encouragement, a disagreeable learning environment, lack of rewards and incentives, loss of confidence and lack of a sense of self-worth.

Whatever the cause, however, it is sobering to appreciate that the further a child progresses through the education system, the wider is the gap between those who learn well and those who are failing; and the more difficult it is for the "failures" to catch up.

Chapter Two

HOW CHILDREN LEARN

Some years ago, I was teaching Colin the names of 3-D shapes:

"What's this?" I asked him, pointing to a cube.

"It's a square," he announced, after a pause, "but it's different."

They usually call it a square before they call it a cube, but Colin had voiced what hundreds before never had – that it was so like a square that you could almost call it that, except that it had depth. Like most four-year-olds (though not by any means all), Colin did not have the vocabulary to define the new object precisely.

"Squarey," Philip, aged five, called those objects.

"What is squarey?" I asked.

"A house is, and a window. And a door. And a TV," he said.

I showed him a wooden cube and square to compare.

"One's squarey, but fatter," he said. In Philip's memory, where all his knowledge is laid out in groups with related meanings, was a group of "squarey" things. Now was the time to be more specific. From a generalised concept ("squarey things"), we moved on to defining 2-D and 3-D objects:

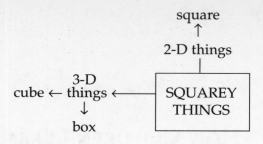

From this group, "house", for example, can be linked to various concrete (real-life objects) and abstract (e.g. home) ideas or concepts.

BUILDING MEMORY

Philip has learnt best, like we all do, by moving from the general ("squarey") to the specific (square, cube). However, the starting point for the whole of shape was not "squarey". It began with Philip as a new-born baby having only perception of shades of dark and light. As he grew up he investigated the demarcation lines between dark and light, finding corners, edges, and getting a sense of "depth" and distance. It is a mechanism for survival, testing and trying the environment and modifying what is already in memory. It leads to the building of larger and larger closely related groups of knowledge.

MATCHING

School learning is not of the survival-related type. It is becoming more artificial as it is becoming more academic.

The relatively efficient process that a baby employs to build knowledge relating to its environment needs to be mimicked when a teacher or tutor presents material for learning. Sometimes, as teachers, we do not fully appreciate how small must be the steps in the mind-building process.

"I can't do this," says Robert, who is nine.

The sum I have given him is $24 + 36 - 29 + 65 = ?$

It is a surprise to me that he finds it difficult. I know that he can add up and take away extremely well. Then, something clicks in my mind:

"Look", I say, "this is really several sums, that you usually write down in a different way."

I write them down :

$$
\begin{array}{r} 2\ 4 \\ +\ 3\ 6 \\ \hline \end{array}
\qquad
\begin{array}{r} 6\ 0 \\ -\ 2\ 9 \\ \hline \end{array}
\qquad
\begin{array}{r} 3\ 1 \\ +\ 6\ 5 \\ \hline \end{array}
$$

His eyes light up, "Easy, peasy, lemon-squeezy," he says.

The knowledge he has in his mind is of sums laid out in the second format. With only the capability of creating a mental image of this, he cannot link to the first format "in a line". Inserting the conversion step allows for translation from one format to the other to occur, and learning can proceed. Robert has matched what enters his mind through his senses with what he now has in memory.

MEANING AND MATCHING

I meet situations like this, when meaning cannot be ascribed to new knowledge, very often, particularly in maths. When what enters through the sense organs (a sight, sound, touch, taste or smell) is not recognised, it is a *non-match* with memory, and in the same league as reading foreign hieroglyphics. A non-match is synonymous with non-meaning for learning (in this context, it is worth remembering that not being able to recall what you know is no different to never having known it in the first place).

Sometimes there is a *complete match* – an eleven-year-old knows immediately the answer to 1+1 = ?. In this case, though, no new learning is occurring. The most effective for learning is a *near* or *close match*, when the new information is recognised as similar to something already learnt.

"That is a semi-detached house," I told four-year-old John. "It's joined to next door. And over there is a detached house. It's not joined to next door."

John's eyes opened wide.

"*That's* what it is," he said. "I thought 'semi-detached' was something different to 'house'."

I could see that he was re-arranging his concept of house, adding the variation of semi-detached and detached.

MIS-MATCH

This is well-illustrated by my experience as a short-sighted eighteen-year-old university student. Starting late for lectures one day, I spotted my bus, a 57, roaring away from the stop, and decided to chase it. After pelting along for four stops I finally caught up, leapt on, and realised that it was a 75. Stepping off with an embarrassed apology to the conductor, I caught a glimpse of his face. It was a picture of open-mouthed, dumb-struck amazement.

Mis-matching is when a child thinks that he or she recognises in learning material, something that has been learnt before. There is a match with the wrong area of memory. Mis-matching particularly occurs when children are dealing with word meanings. I suppose one could write a long book of malapropisms and other misnomers, so common is mis-matching in learning. It arises because the learner is not supplied with material in an image-provoking form (real-life examples, diagrams and drawings are vastly superior to words). It is also the commonest reason for failure with problem-solving, where there is a crying need for children to be taught to dissect a problem into its constituent parts, create images in their minds of these parts, and then re-join them to solve the problem.

The following is a problem that has caused attacks of the horrors to countless bright nine- or ten-year-olds (although adults have little trouble with it):

"There are cows and chickens in a farmyard. If there are 15 heads and 42 legs, how many chickens are there?"

The best way for this age to work this out is to split 15 (trial and error):

Chickens (2 legs)	Cows (4 legs)	Legs
8	7	$8 \times 2 + 7 \times 4 = 44$
etc.		
until 9	6	42 (correct)

Answer: 9 chickens

Nine-year-olds are often unskilled in simple trial-and-error analysis, and often do not have the number bonds for immediate recall ($8 + 7 = 15$, $9 + 6 = 15$, etc). Adults, on the other hand have had much practice over the years through shopping and other real-life experience.

A Pakistani boy, Faisal, virtually tore his hair out over this problem, in spite of being very successful in maths.

MENTAL IMAGES

Central to matching, and therefore to the whole learning process, is the creation of a mental image (picture). Everyday life teaches us that with well-recognised aspects, a match between what we *know* and what we see (or hear, feel, etc) is very fast indeed. When I drive a car, there is no time for dreaming up images, suggesting that matching occurs computer-like through well-used channels. A computer analogue in the mind would be a "recognition unit" that switches on after a certain amount of practice, recognising that the experience being learned is likely to be repeated. At this point, the learnt ability is transformed into what we would term an instinctive skill. There is a quick "scan" for meaning, similar to how we recognise what someone is talking about in a conversation. Practice has made scanning possible, but when we encounter something new, when we need to slow down and consider carefully what we are learning, we strive to create the clearest mental image possible. Time and again, my students (of whatever age) stare into space and strive to create images in their minds so that they can attribute meaning to what they are learning.

This is especially noticeable when they are dealing with spatial maths or any problem solving – trying to locate something in the vast files of memory that can match with what is in front of their eyes. Matthew, aged

16

ten, explained to me how he worked out rotational and bilateral symmetry of 3-D objects so well.

"I take them into my head," he said, "and I turn them round, or chop them in half, just like you do with things at school and at home."

He meant that in his memory were experiences of rotating 3-D objects, of chopping apples and oranges into halves and quarters. When he was asked to determine the symmetry of a shape, he matched the image of the shape with the memory of manipulations of similar shapes in the past.

A Mind-matching System

Learning and memorising are therefore embraced in the computer analogue system, which involves the matching of incoming sensory representation and the images created from long-term memory. Such a system can be represented on a diagram as shown below.

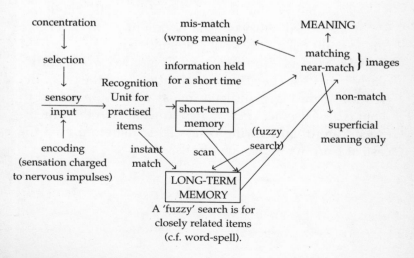

17

AIDS TO VISUALISATION

Clearly a facility to think or dream up clear images gives an advantage in learning. Some children, either through lack of practice in infancy, or because they did not inherit the potential, are less able than others to re-create real-life visions in their minds. For these children, aids to visualisation – real-life experience, drawings, diagrams, clear separation of concepts or learning steps are of great importance.

So called "brighter" pupils have the ability to "imaginify" even from relatively abstract material, or from a "confused" scenario where there are several ideas or items on a page or in a problem. Remedial pupils, on the other hand, find this difficult. Abstract ideas often need to be presented in a concrete way, or skills and structures laid out in clear diagrams. They need to *see* a film portraying jealousy, as opposed to merely having it explained to them. Even with bright pupils, use of these techniques means that learning can be greatly accelerated, or advanced subjects usually taught at an older age can be taught at a very young age indeed.

Slow learners also need carefully graded work, particularly in maths. They find visualisation, and therefore the creation of meaning, difficult unless what is presented to them is an extremely *near* match to what is in their memories. Careful structuring of maths is therefore vital for ease of learning with such pupils.

RECALL

Everything that is learnt, whether it is an item of knowledge, a skill, a process (like multiplying), problem-solving, or, simply, how to think, has to be recallable from memory, or no new learning can take place. A child can understand something perfectly, but if it cannot be recalled fairly easily, progress is stifled.

"She can't remember things," said a teacher about Sonia. "Everything we teach her goes in one ear and straight out of the other."

Sonia did have difficulty with recalling schoolwork, but she startled me by detailing the lives, records and sales – virtually total biographies – of possibly every pop-star living. It sounds like anecdotal evidence for learning through interests, but rather suggests that not enough attention had been given to presenting learning material in a more concrete, real-life way.

"PEGGING" EXPERIENCE

The justification for this view comes from the fact that the great majority of us learn and recall from real-life, with virtually no effort at all. If I visit a street in a strange town, the next day I can remember virtually everything about that street. If somebody famous was there when I visited the street, it is even more memorable. This is because, in my memory, there is entrenched the general concept of a street, with modifications for every street that I have ever visited. Each street modification is "pegged" to time and geographical location (e.g. 10.30 a.m. on 5th June, 1995 in the North-west). Locating time and place is an exercise we have practised from the early years, and the operation is therefore instinctive. I certainly don't need to be *interested* in what I remember about that street, but memorisation is achieved because near-matching is so easy.

The use of "pegs" is widespread in school work – "a" for apple, "b" for banana is one; transforming letters into shapes is another (s-s-s is a snake). "Pegging" is an extremely effective way of rooting "abstract" information into well-used, real-life areas of memory. It facilitates recall.

REPETITION AND PRACTICE

First there is understanding, then recall through pegging, and, finally, repetition to make some aspects of school work instinctive.

Practice has suffered recently from the much-maligned rote repetition of tables. In the past whole classes sat in rows and repeated tables like robots, myself included. It was no trial for me, but possibly for those who had their knuckles rapped with a ruler for not answering quickly enough to "9 eights..?" it was a demeaning and demoralising experience.

Repetition is vital in learning. It turns a learnt skill into an instinctive one: but the *means* to achieve repetition should be as far removed from drudgery as possible. Self-motivation must be strong, and for the very young there should be a strong element of enjoyment. Christopher, who is four, always breaks into his school song for "a,b,c, d..." when I write down the letters for him to copy. Rhymes, jingles and songs to aid learning by repetition are indispensable to the teaching of many aspects of number and language, even for older children.

Salma, who is nine, asked me yesterday, "Why do I have to do these division sums again, when I know how to do them already?"

I explain to her that soon she will be doing harder sums than this (fractions), and that she will not be able to do the new work until she knows division especially well (fraction work involves cancelling which needs good division technique). Just as we practised walking as toddlers – on flat ground, uneven turf, uphill, downhill – until it was steady and instinctive, then moved on to running and leaping, so certain skills must be learnt to "saturation point" before new areas can be conquered.

Chris, who is learning French, begged me to help him with memorising. He was almost in tears. I showed him how to "peg" foreign words ("livres" as "leaves" in "books", idiosyncratically as "leavres"), and then to sit rereading and visualising. Three months later he is gaining top marks, and bubbles with confidence. He also applies the techniques to different aspects of his work.

Points for Improving Learning

1. Through testing, you discover what your child already knows. This will determine what can be taught *immediately* with confidence.

2. Your child must be motivated and focused. The environment must not be a distraction: in general, a child learns best sitting relatively still in a quiet room, with the close encouragement of a parent or tutor. Having said

21

that, my own son at eight would learn sitting at a dining room table with the TV blaring out, and a cacophony of noise as younger brothers ran in and out of the room. Frequent breaks (after about 15 to 30 minutes) are relaxing, and also something to look forward to.

3. Every effort should be made to create as clear a mental image (picture) as possible. A so-called multi-sensory approach is very effective. For example, when teaching phonics, solid letters can be used, their shapes traced in a sand-tray, the sounds of the letters emphasised (s-s-s-s-s-s-snake), and letters can be pointed out in the street, the supermarket, and in books.

4. Such a multi-sensory approach acts as a recall "peg", but idiosyncratic images are best remembered: "I had my breakfast, put 'One' in the cornflakes, 'Two' in my tea and 'Three' in my scrambled egg..." Rhymes like "One, two, buckle my shoe..." serve the same purpose.

5. Repetition or practice performed in as pleasant a way as possible makes skills instinctive, and is invaluable in certain areas.

6. The developing of thinking through problem solving and investigations, and of creativity through conscious effort to link widely separated items of knowledge in memory, must be pursued (see later chapters). Otherwise, a child grows up well-versed in many skills, but is unable to apply them in what is becoming an increasingly important aspect of school work.

Chapter Three

PRE-SCHOOL NUMBER WORK

I find it's a regular occurrence for a proud parent to trot out a small, wide-eyed eighteen-month- or two-year-old who has mastered the rudiments of counting (usually on fingers). So many toddlers learn to count early, and yet so many also go on to have difficulties with school number work.

"I remember Mandy toddling around this room when she was two, chattering to herself and counting on her fingers," said Mandy's mother, quite bewildered that Mandy, at seven years, had just been pronounced severely remedial in school number work. I knew Mandy well. Although she had been precocious as a young child, she was left a lot to her own devices at a pre-school age, and had been at variance with school life for some years.

Mandy certainly *had* been counting at two, but her parents had not capitalised on her obvious intelligence. She had played "outside" mostly before five years of age, and had greatly disliked the restrictions of school. Now aged seven she hardly knew any numbers above fifteen, and had lost confidence in herself. The remedy for her troubles was to help her with her counting and then to move on to addition and subtraction.

Developing Counting

Initially, most parents will have considerable success teaching counting up to three, then on to five. It comes from invoking interest (and visualisation) through real-life objects. You count the steps as you take your child up to bed, count out sweets, cutlery, cookery, chairs, parked cars (an image of a *static* object), houses, objects in picture books.

Sitting your child up at a table and counting five sweets, five buttons for five minutes or so is invaluable. It achieves "focus", and also begins the toddler's perception of "static" learning play as enjoyable – very important for settling into the relatively non-mobile school learning environment.

Playing with Wooden Bricks

A good set of wooden learning bricks is invaluable play-learn material for a pre-schooler. Through a good set (including several equal-sized cubes, cuboids, spheres, prisms, cylinders, cones, pyramids, squares, circles, various triangles – some of wood colour, and others coloured green, blue, red, yellow), your child can sort for colour and shape, can learn to count, add, subtract, and many word meanings (e.g. edge, flat, round, straight, angle, over, under).

Using wooden learning bricks is an important experience for a pre-schooler. The foundation of many aspects of shape in maths, and of perspective and form in art will be laid in his or her memory.

COUNTING RHYMES

"Let me sing you this song from Nursery," says Sofia, aged three-and-a-half (she does this every week). I have to sit still and listen patiently to what feels like 64 verses, with actions. She has perfect pitch and excellent timing, and has learnt all her counting through rhymes like,

"One, two, three, four, five,
Once I caught a fish alive..."
I teach her my own one:
"All good children, count together,
One, two, three, four, five.
(Repeat)
One, two, three, four, five
We're glad we are alive.
All good children count together
One, two, three, four, five."
(Verse 2: *All good children CLAP together*
Verse 3: *All good children STAMP together.*)

"I sing better than you," says Sofia, when I've finished.

Another useful counting rhyme, is to replace "Ten green bottles a'hanging on a wall," with, "Ten teddy bears sitting on a chair", starting with, "One teddy bear," and counting up to ten, and then at, "Ten teddy bears," and going down to one. It's excellent pre-practice for adding and subtraction.

EXTENDING COUNTING

Add two numbers at a time to the ones your child knows and you should be able to get over the counting "sticking point" – the area between twelve and seventeen. Parental

25

disinterest in teaching the teen numbers and above, leads to convolutions at getting to twenty.

"...twelve, thirteen, fifteen, seventeen, eighteen, nineteen, twenty," said Claire, aged three.

Paul, of the same age, was even more succinct:

"...twelve, nineteen, twoty...I think," he declared.

Inadequate grounding in counting leads to failure in number work.

Tracy, at six, learns slowly. I have to build up her addition and subtraction from counting using every possible aid (buttons, a number line). The normal time allotted to being at ease with counting numbers in the Infant School, is not long enough for her. She needs personal attention; but more preferable would have been extensive pre-school counting practice to make re-call more effective. Failure in maths for many slower pupils, starts here. Robert, at eleven, had great difficulty visualising and working with numbers larger than 20. He had been raised in Saudi Arabia until he was eight, and had missed out on grounding work. Apart from this area, though, he was a quick learner.

WRITTEN NUMBERS

Many pre-school children learn to write at least a few of the written numbers (1, 2, 3, 4, 5, for example), and they should be accompanied by the corresponding number of concrete objects:

1 •	2 • •	3 • • •

Drawing numbers on cards with large dots on them creates a good visual image. From time to time, you can stick paper over the dots and ask your child to put the correct number of buttons with the appropriate written number. Your child will give you the lead in how far he or she can go, but, in general, add two numbers when a list is known.

MONEY

The majority of pre-school children count all coins as one unit:

"Look," said Fatima, aged four, "I've got thousands of pounds here." She held up her loaded purse, heavy with a large assortment of coins, both silver and bronze. She tipped them all out on to the table and counted.

"That's 56," she said.

"You can give it to me then," I said, "and I can buy myself the Queen's palace."

"You're not having this money," said Fatima, sweeping it back into the purse. "My mummy's poor, because my dad doesn't give her money to buy new shoes. Now she can get them." Fatima is more astute than she makes out, really. She knows that these coins will buy some sweets, but she also wants to cheer her mum up – so I add a little to her collection.

Now that Fatima can count so well in ones, I can explain how to tap twice on the two unit coin, and five times on a five unit coin:

tap	tap	tap tap	tap tap tap tap tap	
1	1	2	5	is nine

SHAPE

As with all mathematical activities before the age of five, the appreciation of shape is an essential experience. Later work is then more easily grafted on to this knowledge in memory. Although your child sees shapes every day of his life (rectangular, triangular, cuboid, prismatic, spherical), he will not be focused enough to discover properties and basic physical rules that will make corresponding abstract principles easier to grasp in school maths. Play with a wide variety of 2-D and 3-D shapes will achieve this, and also with plasticine or play-doh shapes which can be cut to show symmetry. Cubes can be placed in containers to compare volume. An appreciation of depth can be gained by handling and comparing a square with a cube, and there is a wealth of experience to be gained about angles, rotation and tessellations by drawing round the shapes to make patterns.

Such a wealth of learning can be achieved through play, but some words in association can stimulate interest and begin to build with schoolwork:

1. Names of shapes
It is not necessary to labour over names, but young children are very proud of the knowledge they gain – use cube, square, triangle, circle, oblong (or rectangle).

2. Other useful maths words
Round, straight, half, turn, angle, corner, flat.

These are in addition to extending English word meanings – when comparing weight, length or size for example.

PLAYING WITH THE TILL AND SHOPPING

Shopping is role-play, testing and trying the language and behaviour of adults as shopkeeper and customer. However, little maths is learnt, partly because prices are far removed from the experience of young children. Because they can only visualise small numbers well, I use artificial pricing, and use only one unit coins (three for a teddy, two for a tin of beans, etc.). This makes it easy for the "shopkeeper" and "customer". Later, when two and five unit coins are in use, a situation arises naturally: I caught John (five years) arguing with James (four years).

"I gave him a five coin for that doll. It costs four, and he won't give me any money back," said John.

"That's enough," said James.

John went red in the face. "He doesn't know anything," he complained. "He doesn't even know about change."

"Anyway," said James, "I'm not selling that doll any more."

"You've got to!" John was near exploding. "Shopkeepers got to sell things in their shop, or they get locked up."

I settled the border dispute with a couple of drinks of lemonade and some sweets. Once the change situation had been explained to James, he never looked back.

MEASURING

I have had so much trouble with the measurement of length, weight and volume with school-age children of all ages (up to sixteen years included), that I have to conclude that:

a) The subjects are badly taught in schools

b) There is little "grounding" of concepts in the pre-school years, and

c) There is little understanding of the decimal component of measures.

1. LENGTH

When John was three, I made a cardboard metre "stick", marked off into 100 centimetres, and told him to go and measure the size of the back garden. After half-an-hour, he came back and announced that the garden was 35 metres long and 11 metres wide.

"Why did it take so long?" I enquired.

"Well," he said, shifting from one foot to the other, "I had to find a place so it made the metre stick fit exact."

I knew, then, it was time to explain that it was okay to measure so many metres *and* centimetres left over.

Very few pre-schoolers, though, are this proficient at three; but they still need some foundation in measuring length, and using sticks, "footsteps" or hand-spans is sufficient to compare heights and lengths of various objects.

For example:

"Which is longer – the top of the table, or the rug by the fire?" I asked Annabel, aged four.

She went away, then returned after a few minutes.

"The table top is twenty-three, and the rug is twenty-six," she said. "And a bit more."

"A bit more what?" I asked.

"A bit more of my brother's toy soldier," she said. "It's best for measuring."

Whether your child formally knows metres and centimetres, or simply measures using toys or fingers depends on whether he or she has mastered the general concept (using a standard measure for distance and height), or has moved on to the specific (metres, centimetres, kilometres). At the pre-school age, your child should *at least* appreciate the general idea.

2. WEIGHT

Weight is the second best understood concept of measurement in school, after length (although, a very large number of sixteen-year-olds are not certain whether or not there are 100 centimetres in a metre, 10 millimetres in a centimetre or 1000 grammes in a kilogramme). Pre-school there should be some form of grounding in the use of weighing balances. Using these, your child can play at seeing whether a toy car is heavier than six marbles. Marbles, in fact, are good substitutes for weights:

"I want eight marbles-worth of currants," I told three-year-old Mark. He dutifully did the weighing.

"Marbles make a lot of currants," he said.

3. CAPACITY (VOLUME)

This is the least understood aspect of measurement in school, partly because of lack of practical experience with measuring, but also because of a confusion over terminology. Measuring the same weight (and volume) of water you can get the following results:

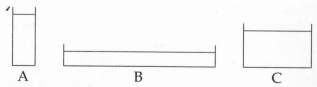

A   B   C

"Which has the most?" I ask Penny, who is four.

"That's the biggest," she says, pointing to A; "but that's the fattest (pointing to C); and that one is squashed (pointing to B)." We can all understand what she is talking about, and it is not along the lines we are trying to lead her. However, when I pour each one into equal sized beakers, she is not really surprised that they are all the same:

"It's a different cup, now," she says, with faultless logic.

Over the years, if you provide your child with a range of plastic cups of various sizes and shapes for water play (in the bath, in the sink), eventually he or she will appreciate what is going on. You can even explain it, this magical effect seemingly at variance with what is seen. The fluidity of liquids can create illusory effects to the untutored eye.

4. TELLING THE TIME

This is a sadly neglected area. Perhaps partly because of the advent of electronic timing, more and more older children are turning up with a complete inability to tell the time (even at fourteen years of age).

To avoid this scenario, at least the hours should be taught pre-school using a play clock with movable hands and clear numbers on the face. You will need to point out that the short hand points to hours. Ideally, a child should also know the half hour position of the hands, the quarter past, and quarter to. A few minutes a day over a few months would easily achieve this, even with a slow learner.

CONCLUSION

Pre-school maths needs to be tailored to school entry, and to the use of abstract symbols. This must not preclude the firm establishing of counting and investigation of shape, however, as the basis of much of early school maths. Only when your child is familiar with counting with concrete objects, and the use of written numbers, should adding and subtraction (with small numbers) be introduced.

It is useful to appreciate that with very little application at all some children sprint into very advanced work indeed. If they enjoy such progress, then they should be given their head.

Chapter Four

PRE-SCHOOL ENGLISH

The educational psychologist bustled into the room. He'd seen it all before – doting parents with a toddler they believed was gifted. He opened his large case and dropped a small pile of wooden bricks on the carpet.

"Let's see you build a bridge," he said to John, who was two and a half.

John began, carefully arranging the bricks to make some complicated structure a little like the Empire State Building.

Eventually, the psychologist lost patience. "Do it like this," he muttered and straddled two bricks by a third.

Mostly on the basis of this, the psychologist pronounced John as an average toddler – in spite of the fact that he had been reading from the age of ten months, could tell the time to the minute and count effortlessly into the hundreds.

I knew what the trouble was. A few days before, I had shown John a picture of the Golden Gate Bridge in San Francisco.

"Is *that* a bridge?" he asked, eyes wide in amazement (the only bridge he'd known was the little "hump-back" in our village). For days afterwards he chattered away about the great bridge, how he'd go there one day and see it in real life.

Then, when the psychologist came and asked him to build a bridge, it was an opportunity to build the "biggest and best".

It is very easy for parents, teachers and psychologists to misinterpret a young child's perception of his world, behaviour and language. At the centre of such misinterpretation are word meanings, and the pre-school age lays the foundation for all of school learning.

David was a very bright boy. He was especially brilliant at maths and science, and eventually took a London degree in maths, getting a first. However, when he was a toddler his mother was distraught, because by three years of age he still hadn't uttered a single word. She'd seen a number of psychologists whose opinions had ranged from the "wait and see" to the "severely mentally impaired". Suddenly, just before four years of age, he talked – and how he talked! He drove his mother half crazy with his chattering. In English at school, though, he never did quite catch up. It is word meanings and phrases learnt before entry to school that can be built on in comprehension work, stories and essays. For example, the concrete word window is a general concept to which can be linked many abstract word meanings:

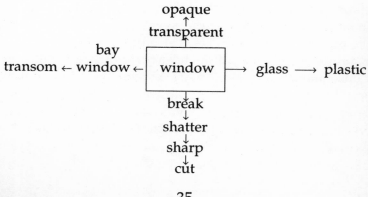

35

Sometimes, adult words sound a little strange when uttered by a small child:

"The gibbon in the zoo," said Sarah, aged four, "has a purple posterior." Mother, aunts and uncles collapsed into hysterical laughter.

"Grandma said I can't say it," said Sarah.

"What?" asked Sarah's mum.

"I can't say 'bottom' in front of all those people on the bus. Especially blue bottom. It's rude, and everybody laughs."

Very adult words uttered by young lips do sound ridiculous, even pretentious, but building a good vocabulary in a pre-schooler often leads to excellent essays later on.

CONCRETE WORDS

Small children learn by repetition, and they learn fast if there are adults or older children to point out objects and name them.

Sam's parents have never communicated properly with him. Pre-school he was left in his older sister's charge, and she was a TV addict (the parents were always unemployed, and spent the evenings "socialising" into the early hours, and the days sleeping). Sam was always playing outside with a host of younger children. Consequently, he lacked word knowledge and certainly could not adapt to the static, abstract world of school. He was good with the snappy, colloquial rejoinder, but all-in-all became a huge problem to both parents and school. He would sit down at home happily and have a story read to him, learn concrete words appendaged to pictures, and even learn counting and addition and subtraction. Contrary to the opinion of his teachers, he was extremely anxious to learn. It was just that life had been unkind and disadvantaged him for school learning.

1. LABELS AND PICTURE CARDS

You can start pre-two using picture books and picture cards to name particular objects that your child sees every day on TV. Although actually seeing a real object is preferable to a picture or a drawing, many children learn about animals not from a zoo visit, but from books. In many Asian households for instance, young children are disadvantaged in word meanings of the country of their birth because they speak Gujarati, Bengali, Hindi, Urdu, etc. with older relatives. One four-year-old, Faisal, surprised me when I was trying to teach him about things being heavy, heavier and heaviest:

"An elephant is heavier than a dog," I said. "Now do you understand what heavier means?"

He looked puzzled. "What's an elephant?" he queried.

I drew him a picture of one.

Faisal grinned in recognition. "I've seen them in *Jungle Book*," he said. "They're friends of Mowgli."

The importance of word meanings cannot be underestimated. The subtitles and nuances of expression can be learned from reading books and conversation, but a vast bank of meanings is built up in the main from having things pointed out.

2. A LIST OF USEFUL CONCRETE WORDS:

table	road (street)	house
chair	shop	car
knife	bus	plate

fork	bus-stop	bowl
spoon	market	cup
bed	sweet	curtain
toilet	chocolate	roof
door	cake	garden
window	tin	

names of fruits	names of vegetables
other things in the house	things in the garden/yard
things at the zoo	things at the sea-side
things at the park	

3. COLOURS

Many children begin to learn their colours between the ages of two and three. Initially, it is best to ignore "shades" and stick to basic colours – blue, green, yellow, orange, red – pointing out, say, objects which are yellow in the environment. To strengthen the image, a yellow colour card can be made using sticky paper over a rectangular piece of card. Gradually, over a period of weeks or months, teach your child one colour at a time, until he knows them all. Failure comes when too many colour names are introduced at the same time, and when reminders are spaced out too widely.

ABSTRACT WORDS

So called concrete words are easy for a child to visualise and thus recall, because they can be easily attached to a picture or real-life object. Abstract words are more difficult because an image is more difficult to link to the spoken (or written) word. However, for all abstract work pictures, diagrams and real-life situations reduce the abstract to the same level as the concrete (in this sense, there is no such things as "abstract", because to divine meaning we must attach an image). Happy, sad, miserable, angry, etc are relatively easy to draw a picture of, but so many school children are unaware of the subtleties in long, longer, longest or fast, faster, fastest, that real-life experience is necessary.

long   _____

longer   _____

longest   _____

Words like "jealousy" are more difficult still. No-one would suggest that your child must be encouraged to experience jealousy to understand it. The solution is to teach the vagaries of human nature through the stories they read, through children's films and videos. Cruella de Ville in "101 Dalmatians" is certainly *cruel*, and the Wicked Queen in "Snow White" is very *jealous*.

Small children listening to a story you read like to talk about the pictures:

"The giant is big, and greedy," said James, aged three, peering at the pictures in the "Jack and the Beanstalk" story.

"He's fierce, too," I said.

I continued reading the story, then stood on a chair and deepened my voice:

"Fee, Fi, Fo, Fum, little children here I come!" I roared.

James's eyes widened in amazement.

"You're just like a giant," he said. "Giants are big and strong and fat."

CONCEPTS

The pre-school years are an ideal time for teaching concepts, but the experiences must be concrete (about real-life things). For example, a tree is a general concept. A very young child will appreciate what a tree *is* if shown a number of different trees (e.g. apple tree, conifer, oak), and if it's explained that "this is its trunk and branches, and leaves. Under the ground are roots going deep down. It's big and has got bark on it." This, of course, is the ideal – to explain exactly what makes up a tree, to examine different trees – an investigation worthy of a sixteen-year-old. Mark, aged four, collected cones, conkers and different shaped leaves from trees:

"Why does that tree have no leaves?" he asked, one bleak winter's day. "That other one has still got its leaves." He pointed to one of the conifers in the back garden. I heaved a sigh. Obviously, I was about to become embroiled in the complexities of "deciduous", "coniferous" and "transpiration" (loss of water from leaves) and many other things.

Mark interrupted my thoughts: "Oh, I know!" he said. "Some trees need to keep warm in winter; so they need leaves."

It had a sort of logic to it, the explanation, so I left it at that and threw in the words "deciduous" and "coniferous". He questioned me for days afterwards, and on every walk and trip to town:

"Is that deciduous?"

"That must be coniferous. It looks warm."

"It's a conifer, because it looks like a triangle."

Building outwards from "tree" to "coniferous/deciduous", and then, eventually to the specific (names of trees, and their characteristics), completes a "group" of knowledge. It is the complete way of learning, and the most effective for recall.

1. OTHER USEFUL GENERAL CONCEPTS TO BUILD ROUND

flower	animal
insect	bird
moving machines (transport)	shop
house (or home)	weather
the seasons	street (or road)
park	

Built into this almost imperceptible learning process are investigations and problem-solving elements. The interest created through these processes will bring immeasurable benefit to progress in school.

READING TO YOUR CHILD

Communicating pleasure in reading can be one of the greatest joys of parenthood. One of the greatest thrills of my life was not in passing my degree, having my first book published, seeing my son pass exams, even seeing my fictional character in a successful TV series – it was watching my two-year-old son reading with lisping, high-pitched enthusiasm the story, "Red Riding Hood", copying all my inflections and characterisations of the Grandma and the wolf: *"What big teeth you have, Grandma!" "All the better to eat you up with!"* Whether or not your child is reading well before five, if you can transmit some of the fascination of books through reading nursery rhymes, poems, fairy stories, picture books to

41

your child, you have a life-long reader on your hands; and reading is an important element in wide ranging academic success.

LEARNING TO READ

To determine readiness to read, you will need to try picture-word cards, and picture books with one picture and word per page. You gradually progress from saying the word with the picture, to asking your child to repeat the word with the picture covered up.

Reading readiness varies from child to child. Most are able to recognise words before the age of five, but beginning to read at three is relatively common amongst quicker learners. I have helped several to read between two and three years and two to read nearer to one year. One child recognised words at ten months of age.

The reason for such a wide variation must include inherited abilities, but undoubtedly many children are held back because their readiness to read is not recognised. Parents continually say to me, "We thought that pre-school time was a time for play." Learning about books and learning to read should be approached as an extension of play, and as long as encouragement rather than coercion is the order of the day, early reading should not be denied.

A child, for example, able to enjoy reading for herself at two is simply not fulfilling her potential if she is not introduced to books until five years of age. Apart from the reading itself, the knowledge of word meanings, spellings, sentence structure, etc at an early age, is a solid foundation on which schoolwork can be built.

1. PHONICS

This usually begins with the A-B-C, although it should be learnt as "a" for apple, "b" for banana, and so on. Many parents lay much emphasis on teaching the alphabet to their children. Unfortunately, it is taught in a rote way and lends nothing to pre-reading. Taught as phonics it is very valuable. The difficulty is in making it interesting to a pre-school child. After years of experimenting with changing into a boot and so on, which has been pretty effective, I have now graduated on to making up stories for each of the letters e.g. how "a" grew into an apple, and "b" the boot went shopping one day, especially if the story is funny.

Many parents teach the phonic alphabet "straight" (with pictures), usually to children aged between three and four and a half. It is probably best to teach four letters at a time, spending only a few minutes each day over a few months.

WRITING

To give your child a clear advantage when starting school, it is important that the rudiments of writing have been tackled (mainly between the ages of three and five). Gloria, a West Indian girl, was very adept physically. Her mother taught her at two years of age how to hold first a crayon, and then a pencil. She was very interested in drawing, good at sketching out both curves and straight lines. When I started tutoring her, she was three and could reproduce virtually all the alphabet lower-case letters with ease. Her grandmother, a very patient lady, had by gentleness and kindness trained Gloria to write. In addition, Gloria turned out to be an extremely quick learner in more intellectual avenues.

Speed of learning and artistic ability/handwriting do not always go hand-in-hand, though. James, an exceptionally gifted artist from a very young age, produced beautiful handwriting, but was considered remedial in maths and English. It was a question of focus. His parents, particularly his mother, encouraged him in what she perceived was James's over-riding talent. There may even have been some vicarious element. Whenever James was hounded for more effort in maths and English, James's mother supported his insistence that he did not need to succeed in these directions.

"Why don't they give him prizes on Speech Day for his artistic success, for his handwriting, instead of highlighting his academic failures?" she moaned. I did point out that James would be happier if he did succeed to some extent in other subjects. From being a bullied and teased boy, he would gain some pleasure from friendships with boys of his own age.

Being good at handwriting includes slow learners and fast learners: but everyone benefits from a gentle introduction to letter shapes pre-school, usually as part of drawing or painting play.

A FOUNDATION FOR SUCCESS

Although some children will learn to read well, to write well and even to spell before entering mainstream school, the aim of early English education must be to develop a wide and varied "bank" of word meanings in the memory, to develop a love of reading (or being read to), and to develop the skill of writing so that at least a few letters can be written down. A knowledge of the phonic alphabet would be invaluable. Such development before school age would allow abstract school work to link more easily to memory.

Chapter Five

INFANT MATHS
(FIVE TO SEVEN YEARS)

The transfer from concrete maths to the use of abstract symbols causes virtually all the problems for this age group. Most children learn to count well using real-life objects and pictures, but remembering the written numbers is a problem:

"It's six," says Sofia, aged five, counting a line of elephants. "How do you write 6?"

I write out 1, 2, 3, 4, 5, 6, 7, 8, 9, 10 at the top of the page, and Sofia is happy, although she keeps losing her place as she counts along the line of written numbers. This means that she is still having difficulty recalling that number of images at one time from memory. I reduce the number to 5, and she romps away.

The difference between Sofia and Ahira, also aged five, is considerable. Ahira can visualise extremely well, and learns the written number line very easily, whereas Sofia needs step-by-step consolidation.

"I'm bored with this," says Ahira, if the progress is too slow.

"All right," I say, "I'll make the number line longer." Then, she is happy again.

Both girls must be taken through the same steps,

graded (prerequisite) but Ahira can visualise and recall much better. However, if a step is missed, even she fails.

STEPS IN BASIC MATHS

There is no *absolute* order of steps. Switching order around can suit one child better than another. However, the following order is highly preferable.

1. COUNTING

Learning to count without using written numbers, and using real-life objects is very important. With my own sons I used an abacus, ten rows of ten. Wooden cubes are also useful, as are cards with pictures on.

Counting *must* be the first in any order, and your child must realise that each unit in counting *must* be the same (e.g. a line of elephants, a line of triangles).

2. WRITTEN NUMBERS

It is best to step-down in numbers here, and teach one to five only, in concert with counting.

l	ll	lll	llll	lllll
1	2	3	4	5

In a remedial set at school, Lilifer, aged eleven, has been taken back to counting with real-life objects:

"I haven't done this since I was a baby," she complains (meaning when she was five). The real difficulty for her, though, is the transfer to *abstract* symbols, in particular the inability to "see" a written number as representing several real-life objects.

The answer, as for most of my students, is to lay out a page with written numbers and counting sums:

● ● ● ●   4

* * *   3

x x x x x   5

– – – – –   5

● ●   2

Later, the numbers can be extended to 10, to 15, to 20, to 25, to 30.

It is extremely important to extend counting before pressing on with advanced addition and subtraction. I have had to take Sofia (now aged six) *back* to counting beyond 15 because she is not well grounded enough for more advanced addition and subtraction.

AIDS TO COUNTING

For those children who cannot visualise well (that is, those who keep saying, "I can't remember what to do in this"), it is extremely useful always to provide a number line at the top of a page of sums:

```
 0    1    2    3    4    5    6    7    8    9   10
 |____|____|____|____|____|____|____|____|____|____|
```

Even better, is to arrange the line vertically with 10 at the top.

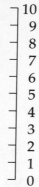

James has used his ruler as a number line for some time now. At the beginning (as with many early learners), I have had to explain that "1" on a number line is the distance between 0 and 1 or 1 and 2, etc. This becomes very important for addition and subtraction later on.

Many Asian children count on the "gaps" between the creases over the joints on their fingers. Using these, there are 28 spaces on two hands – it is an abacus you *have* to carry everywhere with you (obviously, the fingers are good for early counting, but with limited range). Fatima was always using her toes to do addition and subtraction beyond 10 (a natural thing to do, because she was always walking around bare-footed).

Aids to strengthen the image in the mind must be continued as long as possible, especially for slower learning pupils.

ADDING SUMS

As with counting, there are several concepts (ideas) involved in simple addition. Step-wise building needs to be carefully attended to, and consolidated.

1. USING REAL OBJECTS
Put two piles of counters/buttons/conkers on the table, and get your child to count the separate piles, then push the piles together and count the total. This will create a mind picture of what adding *is*. Use numbers less than five:

"This is a good game," said Mark, aged five. "What is it for?"

"It's called adding," I said.

"It's silly, really," said Mark. "You should put them all together first, then count them."

"It's useful," I said, "when your cousin (who lives 10 miles away) has some conkers, and you have some. So you phone him, to see how many you've got altogether."

"I don't want to know what *he's* got," said Mark. "I've always got more than him anyway."

2. USING WRITTEN NUMBERS AND AIDS
Cards are useful

| . | | . | makes | . | . |

and leads on to:

| . | and | . . | makes | . | . | . |
| 1 | | 2 | | 3 | | |

Thereafter, appendage dots to each number :

$\overset{\cdot}{1} + \overset{\cdot\cdot}{2} \to \overset{\cdot\cdot\cdot}{3}$

and

$\overset{\cdot}{1} + \overset{\cdot\cdot}{2} = \overset{\cdot\cdot\cdot}{3}$

Consolidating this stage well, and keeping numbers small, is extremely important. Failure in numbers often has it roots in failure at this stage.

More than is a totally different concept to add, so has to be explained using wooden bricks with subtraction:

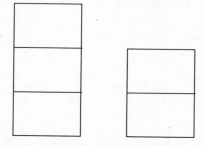

one *more* to make them the same

3. NUMBER BONDS

Practice with numbers up to five is important:

$2 + 3 = 5$ $4 + 1 = 5$ $0 + 5 = 5$

I gave Sofia $2 + 3 = ?$

"You've done that already," she said, pointing to $3 + 2 = 5$. "It's the same, isn't it?"

I pointed out that $1 + 4$ was the same as $4 + 1$, $5 + 0$ the same as $0 + 5$.

"It's all lemon-squeezy," she said.

She continued looking for patterns, and found them useful later in multiplication – 2 x 3 is the same as 3 x 2 (if a child doesn't know the three times table, and knows the two times table, it speeds the solution).

4. EXTENDING ADDING

Whether addition is extended before teaching simple taking away is a personal choice. I have tended to teach subtraction with small numbers straight after addition with small numbers, and to build the two up together.

The number line is invaluable with bigger numbers (count up for adding, down for subtraction). It is also important to realise that doing sums up and down creates a different image from take away horizontal, so both arrangements should be learnt from the beginning :

Add ⌐ 10
─ take
─ away
─ ↓
⌐ 0

```
 ...    ..  .....
 3  +  2  = 5            3 ...
                       + 2 ..
                       ───────
                         5 .....
```

5. RESOURCEFUL COUNTERS

Alan, at six, has learnt to count the numbers round the clock. He adds by first counting one number, say four, to 4 o'clock, then restarting and adding, say three, from the 12 as "5, 6, 7," round to 3 o'clock.

Ahira, aged five, amazed me yesterday by doing her adding up using pens and pencils. This is entirely unprompted, and is a technique of visualising recommended to foreign language students for learning foreign phrases. In Ahira's case, she counts one number in her mind on one coloured pencil, then counts the addition on another of a different colour. The pencil acts as a containment unit for each counted number.

TAKING AWAY

As with adding, a good foundation must be laid using buttons, sweets, fingers and taking one away:
000   remove 0
leaves 2

Using only numbers up to five seals the concept in memory.

When it comes to using the written numbers, confusion reigns. The symbols do not align with the concrete activity, because you cannot divide up the written three and take one away. It is possible to insert a step:

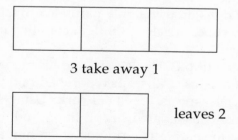

3 take away 1

leaves 2

However, it is a long stride to:
3 - 1 is 2
and needs appendaging dots:
3 - 1 = 2
... - .   = ..

It is a classic illustration of the difficulty of relating abstract display to a perfectly understood concrete activity. Initially, the dots need to be crossed off for a child, or linked to using fingers. It requires practise to bridge the gap effectively. An abacus helps, although the aim eventually is to be more facile and work away from the concrete link.

TIMES TABLES

An abacus is invaluable here, too. A 10 x 10 abacus can be used to count in twos up to at least 20. The two times table is best learnt and used as the basis for teaching simple multiplication and division. Initially, the two times table can be learnt as 2, 4, 6, 8... but great benefit can be gained by learning the table as:

1 x 2 = 00   2
2 x 2 = 00 00   4

Many of the problems I encounter come from rushing on to new tables too quickly, and trying to teach multiplication and division using only partly learnt tables.

Wooden cubes are also useful for counting in twos and for sharing.

Asif used buttons. He was six, and his mother was trying to improve his maths. His report had said that he was "poor" at all aspects of schoolwork. Using buttons as counters we consolidated his addition and subtraction, moving on to sharing (sharing between him and myself using the buttons) and he raced on. He was an astonishingly quick learner. Later he could divide using brackets:

2)‾10̅   "How many twos in ten?"

The question provided the link between the two times table and the symbols for division. In end of term tests he came top in maths (*this*, on one hour tuition per week).

1. SMALL NUMBERS
There are very definite links between adding and multiplication (the two times table is adding twos), and between multiplication and division:

$$3 \xrightarrow{\times 2} 6$$
$$\xleftarrow{\div 2}$$

Only when a concept has been learnt beyond "saturation" or "overlearning" point using *small* numbers, should "big" numbers be introduced. Visualisation is far easier with small numbers where young children are concerned. This does not preclude teaching "counting on", but subtraction and addition using large numbers (e.g. 19 - 8 and 17 + 9) should be taught with the appropriate number line nearby. When multiplication and division are well understood, and *well practised* using the two times table, only then should the ten times and the five times tables be taught and used.

"Brilliant! Well done!" I said to Claire, aged six, who had just completed a full page of mixed sums, including multiplication and division. At five, Claire had been morose, aggressive and having problems at school. Her teacher had been complaining about her behaviour, and she was learning very little. Now, at six, she is top and a happy, contented and extremely likeable girl. She is an example of a child "caught" at just the right time – without the help she almost certainly would have been a case for remedial help, a failure, and more important, *feeling* a failure.

MONEY

Ahira can count well (at five), so the other day I drew a
line of coins, showed her how to tap twice on two unit
coins, five times on five unit coins and laid out some
sums:

5	2			is	?
5	2	2		is	?
2	2	2	1	is	?
10	5	5	1	is	?

She is a very quick learner, so I made the counting difficult. She raced through the sums, then, on the last asked:

"How do you write twenty-one?"

A little return to basic counting numbers was required:

"It's easy now," she said. "I want hard sums."

"Hard" sums she will get; just that little bit "harder" to
cause a near-match and build.

Chapter Six

INFANT ENGLISH
(FIVE TO SEVEN YEARS)

Success at this age depends very much on whether a solid foundation has been laid pre-school. A good foundation includes an interest in learning, being used to sitting down to learn, a wide experience of words and their meanings, an interest in books, being versed in the rudiments of reading (phonic alphabet, word shape – sound recognition, etc), and being able to write letters. The most successful have been taught to read, can write well and can converse on a wide range of subjects with adults. They do not suffer from any disadvantage emotionally for being taught pre-school, and keep ahead throughout school life. They are highly socially orientated and co-operative as a rule, learn fast on top of what they already know, yet derive great benefit from investigations and other practical work. The only difficulty for such children is when misguided egalitarian pressures try to hold down their progress to the lowest common denominator:

"We can't have some children getting ahead of the others and making them feel inferior," said one head-mistress.

One Asian mother was shouted at because she had taught her daughter to read before school:

"We decide when a child begins to read," snarled the teacher.

The dislike of some teachers for the occasional gifted child is illustrated by Simon, a seven-year-old in my class who was far ahead of the others in English and maths. This was an area of back-to-back terraced houses, and Simon lived on the fringe of the area in a large detached house. Others in the class were average learners and there were about 17 Ugandan Asians, most of whom could hardly read. The previous teacher disliked Simon intensely. He was "a snob, and big-headed," she said, and she refused to single him out for special treatment. I did, though, setting him work commensurate with his level of attainment. He settled down happily, with individually targeted work, while I set about teaching the Ugandans to read. "Clashes of personality", so-called, between teachers and particular pupils, figure largely in failure. Sometimes the child is used to having too much of his or her own way at home, and resents a teacher's domination. Such a situation can only then be resolved by enlisting the parents' backing in explaining that he or she is only one of many in the classroom, and must be treated equally. Sometimes, sad to say, it is the teacher who needs to examine his or her feelings and behaviour.

READING

The above example of having seventeen non-readers, aged eight, and from a foreign country in one's classroom, none of whom was speaking this country's language at home, is unusual. However, between September and Christmas, and using an excellent graded reading scheme, I managed to teach all those seventeen to read from very well to fairly well. I am sceptical of talk of children resistant to learning to read. It is true that I had to set work for the rest of the class while I spent five minutes every day with every pupil (meaning that I was spending over two hours every day on reading alone). The justification is that a child who cannot read well by eight is going to lose out all the way down the line – bad spelling, bad punctuation, bad stories, bad essays, failure in problems, failure in related or dependant subjects (e.g. history, geography, science, even maths investigations).

1. WILL NOT READ(ERS)

Distinct from the non or weak readers are a great body of children who will not read, much to many a parent's disgust. The "turn-off" is most noticeable amongst boys who are lured away by sports and games outside, computer games or videos. However, that is not the whole answer because for 20 years now I have tried to discover the antidote to "boring" books and stories. Local libraries and school libraries are full of books, but many just do not appeal to the boys and girls they are aimed at.

"Please," begged Asif aged seven, "I've tried all the books in the school library, and they're *so* boring."

Asif is a highly intelligent boy. He is desperate to read. I suggested Enid Blyton's "Famous Five", and he was caught:

"I read one book as soon as I get it, then read it again straight away," he said. Now, his father is complaining that he can't get him to turn off his light at night!

Chris is another. He graduated from the adventure stories of Enid Blyton at seven, to the gruesome stories of Roald Dahl. Now, at eleven years of age he has "discovered" Arthur Ransome and is wading through book after book.

"Where are all the stories about magic and witches?" asked Salma. She had found a few, but too many Real Life stories about "Issues".

Children want to read, but as one educationist explained:

"The difficulty comes when, between the reader and the writers, are groups of people not up-to-date with what the reader wants." Adults since Victorian times have sought to impose their taste on children, and have always notoriously mis-read children's reading taste.

I have, therefore, to advise parents to try certain books and writers that I know many children adore. Like me, you will have to divine your child's interest and *search*. Mark, at seven, for instance, is fascinated by nature, and story books about animals absorb him for hours.

For slower readers, picture books are the answer, with few words and a good dash of humour.

2. NON-READERS

Non-readers should be readers by six or seven, or you have a school failing. If your child is beginning to read, however, you can help by reading and re-reading through his school reader when he brings it home. You can also supplement with phonic work as explained in pre-school English; and, also, find some easy-read rhyme, story books or picture books from the library or book shops. One book can be re-read many times, once or twice an evening. The stories are important – five and six year-olds love to read fairy stories that they have heard before. Make sure words are printed big, and that there are few words on each page (one or two lines at the most). Books using Key Words (words that occur most commonly in text) are very effective; and some children show startling progress if words are written out on flash cards. These are best appendaged to a picture where possible:

Other words are learnt best if the structure is pointed out, or letters traced in the air (e.g. is, the, and).

Closing the eyes, visualising the word shape and saying the word simultaneously also results in good retention and recall.

EARLY WRITING

Regular practice at copying the letters is essential (about five minutes daily). If your child can write the letters, then, like Amy, she can practice writing short sentences, putting her finger down to gauge spaces between the words:

"It's hard," she says.

"I know," I say.

"It's boring," she continues. "Why do I have to do writing?"

"Well, you can be a doctor one day, or, maybe, a writer."

"I want to be a writer like you," she says. "I'll be famous and rich."

"Not necessarily."

She works away like a beaver, one of a solid band of a million schoolgirls, each of whom is about to embark on her personal masterpiece. Some lucky editors are going to get them one day, piled high on their in-trays.

Start with the letter "O", then the "C". Guide your child's hand if she finds it hard going.

1. FIRST STORIES

These can start as a few words written beneath pictures he or she has drawn:

This is my dad
by Mike

Write down the words for copying either directly on the drawing sheet, or on a separate sheet.

As schools have realised, writing a daily diary is one way of extending writing. Writing down stories they have heard (e.g. "Snow White", "Red Riding Hood") is another. A few words, or a couple of sentences is enough at first.

2. SPELLING

When a child can read and is aware of letter sounds (phonics), simple three-letter words can be learnt in related groups, e.g. man, can, pan, ran.

(These are given in the tests section, for reference).

Chapter Seven

JUNIOR MATHS
(SEVEN TO ELEVEN YEARS)

Lilifer is eleven. She is tall and big for her age, and noisy when excited. She also lacks confidence in academic work. I show her how to do carrying in adding, and she jumps up and claps her hands:

"I know! I know," she squeals. "It's easy! Easy!"

The school is devoted to practical work, which is fine; but at some point the transfer to abstract "paper and pencil" work needs to be achieved. Referring constantly back to real-life is not always possible in maths. In a sum like 61 - 42, a pupil may be aware that a "ten" needs to be "borrowed" from experience in practical work, but for further operations to be learnt, the *skill* of abstract subtraction needs to be taught. A whole body of language is built up in maths which cannot easily be referred back to real-life (use of larger numbers, algebra, etc).

Near-matching is achieved, and thus learning, by carefully building, step-wise, operation on operation (e.g. multiplication built on addition). Operations, after explaining their meaning through basic practical work, are visualised, and a new operation and its meaning built into it.

"BIG" NUMBERS

New concepts in numbers are usually learnt using *small* numbers, because these are easily visualised. However, many of the problems at this age arise because of inability to visualise large numbers:

"What's half of ten?" I ask Alison, who is seven, and a quick learner.

She turns away and stares at some distant point, visualising a ten number line.

"Five," she says very definitely.

"What's half of one hundred?" I ask.

She looks at me, making no attempt to visualise. She knows that big numbers present a muddled picture in her mind.

"Is it twenty?" she asks, a pleading look coming into her eyes.

At an older age (nearer eleven), Andrew has trouble "chopping" 1000 into portions. He can easily do it with 100, but the expanse of 1000 defeats him.

To enable visualisation (without writing out hundreds of numbers), arrays are very effective.

1. A HUNDRED ARRAY

1	2	3	4	5	6	7	8	9	10
11	12	13	14	15	16	17	18	19	20

etc.

This can be used in conjunction with the 10 x 10 abacus to show tens and units (10 + 2 = 12), patterns (67 + 10 = 77, 77 + 10 = 87, etc,) and table patterns:

1   2   3   4 $\boxed{5}$ 6   7   8   9 $\boxed{10}$

Using the array is probably the best way of visualising times tables. It also enhances the ability to add and subtract with numbers up to 100, for extended adding or subtraction of the type: 65 - 9, 74 + 8.

2. CARRYING
Faisal is confused about a sum. He adds it like this:

```
    T    U
    2    7
+   1    4
  ─────────
    3    11
```

He also adds the left line first (any teacher of seven-year-olds will instantly recognise the scenario).

It is most important that, using "ten" strips of cards, your child works in concert with the abstract symbols. This provides the visualisation for the link.

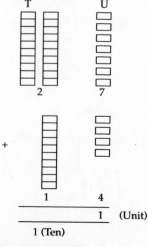

65

Sometimes, practical grounding in tens and units makes the whole thing incomprehensible. Lilian does not understand that :

12   is

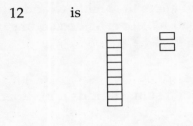

1 ten   2 units

A whole host of troubles would be avoided if so-called "place-value" was explained properly early on. As with all things, some children learn very quickly. Others, eager not to be seen as out of touch say they do, but the "picture" is not clear. The difficulty with understanding place value lasts way into the teens.

Using symbols *with* the practical work is vital – we are trying here to build abstract processes on to the central, mainly practically conceived, idea of tens and units:

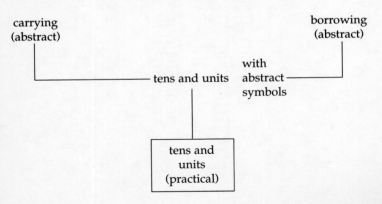

When grounding is sufficient, there will be no more of Faisal's bewilderment:

"What carries underneath, is it the one or the three?" (for 13).

3. BORROWING

Again, the practical use of card or paper "tens" used in conjunction with the sum is important. This is a teeth-grindingly slow process, best done on an individual basis. Basically, it is what Martin, aged seven, called "fiddly", and for this reason alone hinders the production in the mind of a clear image. Gradually, however, light dawns, slower in some minds than others, though.

$$
\begin{array}{cc}
\text{T} & \text{U} \\
23 & 1\!\!\not{2} \quad (10 + 3 = 13) \\
\underline{-15} & \underline{-1 \qquad 5} \\
\underline{} & \underline{}
\end{array}
$$

WELL DONE!

TELLING THE TIME

Working in people's homes, when it comes to teaching the time, I ask to borrow a toy clock, or a bedroom alarm clock with easy-to-move hands. Sometimes, I wish desperately for the "perfect" teaching aid, one that would iron out all problems: a clock with the numbers marked clearly (not Roman numerals!). At the number 3 it says also quarter past, at 6 is says half-past, at 9 it says quarter to. Also, the minutes are marked clearly and there is some system of showing five minutes at the number 1, ten at the number 2, etc. Learning the time brings on to some children's faces an expression of intense horror:

"*Not* the clock!" squealed Fatima, aged six, as if it was some medieval torture.

Yet, if the various elements are spread over a period of time, even very young children can learn to tell the time. It is simply a matter of a parent taking time out to sit (with a good teaching clock) for five minutes every evening. The sequence of learning is:

(i)   O'clock, half hour, quarter past, quarter to.
(ii) Counting round the clock in fives.
(iii) Setting the hands to "*past* the hour" times, and testing over a period.
(iv) "*To* the hour" times.
(v) The much vexed question of what does 1.45 mean? (i.e. it is the same as a quarter to two, or 15 minutes to two.)
(vi) Asking how long from, say, 1.15 to 1.35 (using the clock still – *within* an hour first).

The final phase is learning, for example, 'How long from 11.30 to 2.45'. This seems to be badly taught in schools, for

68

I have had countless numbers who find this difficult (all the way up to sixteen years of age). Salma's teacher, however, has taught her well. At eight she, an average child, can do the following calculation.

How long from 11.30 to 2.45? The sum is easy if these are followed:

	hours	mins
Write down:		
(i) from 11.30 to 12.00		30m
(ii) from 12.00 to 2.00	2h	
(iii) from 2.00 to 2.45		45m
Total	2h	75m

75 minutes is 1 hour 15 minutes

So, finally	3h	15m

Learning to tell the time is difficult for a child to visualise unless it is broken down into these steps.

Other exercises that extend ability in this area are :

(i) Turn 2 hours 5 mins into minutes.
(ii) Turn 140 mins into hours and minutes.

To do these, your child will need the following table written down:

Hours	Minutes
1	60
2	120
3	180
4	240

69

EXTENDING MULTIPLICATION AND DIVISION

As soon as a child learns and understands the two times table, multiplication and division can be advanced.

Philip cannot grasp multiplication. Somewhere along the line he has been rushed on to multiplying without being shown how it relates to a times table, the *meaning* of 3 x 2, of the abstract symbol x. He knows it is not 3 + 2, but what is it?

	3 x 2	is	..	+	..	+	..	
and	5 x 2	is	..	+	..	+	..	+ .. + ..

5 x is fifth along the table:

2	4	6	8	10	12	14	16	18	20
				↑					
1	2	3	4	5	6	7	8	9	10

Practice with adding twos and pin-pointing the sum on the table line is vital, visualising the two times table on the fingers.

Two weeks later, Philip is faced with: 3
                                   x2

instead of 3 x 2   ——

This step is important because the image of the vertical sum is different to the horizontal one. Although he is used to adding vertically, tables are usually written horizontally. In learning, the close-match step must be found to advance successfully (the new "picture" must be easy to make).

For this reason certain sums are learnt better if broken down into steps:

```
  13  is two sums   1   and   3
 x 2                x2         x2
 ──                 ──         ──
 ──                 ──         ──
```

DIVISION IS EASIER

As a teacher, my education lecturers had carefully explained that children find division more difficult than multiplication. I believed that implicitly, until John announced that division was a lot easier than multiplication.

He was right. For the sums:

$$2 \overline{)\ 12} \quad \text{or} \quad 12 \div 2$$

read "How many twos in 12?"

Even without the two times table it is easy for Philip to work out:

```
       6
  2 ) 12
.. .. .. .. ..
 1  2  3  4  5
```

After Philip is clear with this he moves on to remainders:

```
      1    r1
  2 ) 3
```

Always consolidate learning with the two times table, and with small numbers.

"Maths is easy," says Philip, aged eight. "It used to be hard, now it's easy."

Finally, Philip is faced by:

$$2 \overline{)\,36}^{\,18}$$ The remainder is carried.

"You can do really hard sums now, Philip," I tell him. He is thrilled – so am I. Philip is a slow learner. By eight he understands the basics of numbers. He is going to do well at maths now, partly because he does know the basics, and partly because his teachers will perceive that he is capable.

FRACTIONS

Karen, aged eight, has been taught the meaning of a half. So, she knows how to share eight sweets between two children.

"They each got half," she says.

I lay out eight sweets:

"Half of eight is four," and separate two groups of four.

We then try examples with different numbers of sweets (10, 12, 6, 4) until the link between sharing with two, and 'a half' is established.

"It's like the two times table," she says, suddenly.

Now comes a very important link that when missing causes much failure in Junior School maths. Working out half of a number by practically sharing is fine when numbers are small, but we need to establish this link for halving *large* numbers.

"What is half of 50?" I ask, suddenly. Karen looks

blank. Up to this point she has happily been able to visualise separating groups of eight sweets, ten sweets and so on. Now she can't do it.

"It's the same as dividing by two," I say. "Half of ten is five, ten divided by two is five..." Eventually we get around to:

$$2 \overline{\smash{)}50}^{\,25}$$

(Karen has learnt to divide well – a prerequisite to fraction work.)

This sequence shows again that as a new concept is being learnt, there must be a careful building out from a closely related concept. In this case, Karen *knows* what sharing is, she knows what a half is, and she is aware of division. Each of these concepts creates a clear image in her mind, and she can recall these images at will. The difficulty is in establishing links so that she can "chop" 50 in half by division. Later she will modify her vision of halving numbers to 100 and well beyond. As many adults do, she will be able to visualise and chop in half 1000, 5000, or, even, 500,000; and when the halving is difficult – say, half of 765,426 – she has recourse to division.

There are several important aspects to the mechanism of learning illustrated here.

1. A new experience must be closely related to something already learnt.

2. For good recall, there needs to be a period of practice with the new experience, constantly referring back to what is being built on to (e.g. when learning half of eight,

keep referring back to sharing). The creative element of linking already established concepts (e.g. division, sharing, fractions) together, will increase Karen's ability to cope with various aspects of this area of maths. She is becoming a creative, thinking, mathematician.

3. The whole process is "fiddly", and time consuming – one reason why this particular subject is one of the main failure areas in maths. Working with maths and science pupils up to university entrance level, I am often shocked at their weakness in the area of ratio. It starts here, with fraction work. A gap or hole has been left in the vast web of the interconnections of memory.

Chapter Eight

JUNIOR ENGLISH
(SEVEN TO ELEVEN YEARS)

By the age of seven the gap between those who are succeeding and those who are failing has widened considerably. Over the years I have found ranges of attainment in children that extend from those who cannot read a single word, to those who can read anything put in front of them. This would seem to suggest that the former have some severe mind problem that hinders learning, and that the latter have some almost magical ability to consume learning material.

This is not so. Not taught correctly, the quick learners tend to stagnate learning-wise, and with purposeful attempts to achieve focus, the failures begin to succeed. The difference is in the input needed to get some children to learn as opposed to others. This means that some children will always languish behind others, but, hopefully, not too far behind.

A sense of failure in children comes from the feeling that they are in a hopeless, no-win situation. Others are far ahead – they can recall well, they can spell well, and they are going even further ahead. It is like a race against an opponent who runs on far ahead until he disappears over the horizon. What is the point in trying to catch up? Lack of motivation adds to the "failure gap" between the succeeders and the failures.

FAST AND SLOW

Since slower learners need considerably more input and attention to keep up with fast learners, this means that fast learners in school can end up being side-lined as far as attention is concerned.

This leads to the situation where fast-learners are failing with respect to their potential; and they certainly recognise that they are getting less attention than the slow learners. Stephen resorted to pretending that he could not do things so that he would get the attention of his teacher. In fact, he was an extremely fast learner, and had behavioural problems because he was frustrated and bored.

On a one-to-one basis Stephen, with hardly a glance at the work I gave him, would say:

"I can't do that."

"Stephen," I said, "I know you can do this. You're not to trick me."

He smiled. "All right," he said, and proceeded to complete the work at rocket-like pace.

Back at school the problems persisted, though. One reason was that he has friends among the slow learners, and was afraid of being "too clever" for them.

"Ben can't do things," he said about one of his friends. "I help him with his reading."

"Then, Ben *knows* that you're cleverer, and he doesn't mind," I said. "He likes you because you're an interesting boy."

With help at home, Stephen did develop astonishingly. He rivalled the best in his class in reading and spelling; but he kept his friendship with Ben way into his teenage years.

Ben, on the other hand, an extremely amiable boy, did

not visualise words and sounds well. At eight his reading was well behind, and he could spell little more than one syllable words. To enhance his spelling, unlike Stephen, he needed pictorial enhancement using diagrams, and the careful grouping of words:

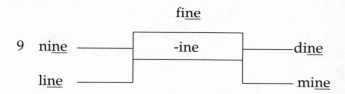

Where possible, introducing a picture to accompany a word helped considerably. However, drawing representations of words like "dine" and "mine" need skilled artistry, and it takes time for all abstract words to be represented so. One day, I dream, the perfect learning system will include all words grouped according to *shape* and also *sound*, cross-linked, and with a linked image. This could certainly be achieved through a computer disk, mimicking perfectly the set-up in memory:

Such a system would enable the slow learners to learn as fast as many fast learners learn now. Fast learners, however, would also benefit, but the disparity between fast and slow learners would not be so great.

The sense of failure in children would all but be eliminated.

77

OLDER FAILURES FAIL EARLY

All the elements must be right if failure is to be turned into success.

Without the ability to read, and an *interest* in reading, many children's English suffers from this point throughout their whole school life.

Gary, at seventeen years, is a quick learner approaching university entrance. In English, though, he is failing. He spells badly, and his knowledge of word meanings is surprisingly low for such a capable boy. He fights with himself to even attempt the exercises I set him.

"So boring," he says, with obvious distaste. He admits, though, that when he was in Infant and Junior School he was a tearaway.

"They let me do nothing," he says, "so I got behind. Then it was hard to catch up."

He never got into the habit of reading, and played outside a lot. This is a scenario that I find with many teenage boys – active outside, playing – who have never tuned in to even the short periods of learning needed to sustain success. They often get motivated late into their teens and struggle to catch up. One boy of fourteen was considered hopeless, and languished in the remedial seventh set. Working with him for just one hour per week, by the time he was sixteen he was on a par in maths with top set pupils. He passed exams with high grades. English, though, was more difficult to promote than maths, simply because a good pupil in English has learnt so much more than the poor pupil. In maths, with skilled mind building, a low achieving pupil can catch up relatively quickly.

REGULAR, PERSISTENT HELP

Andrew was a failure when he was nine, 28th out of 30 in his class. His spelling was poor, and he never read a book voluntarily. I worked with him for one hour per week. His spelling improved only gradually over the years, but by sixteen he achieved top grades in English. Now, at eighteen, he has won an engineering place in university with good science and maths grades. His father and mother are proud of him – they never "achieved anything at school". Andrew is also a quick learner and always does the minimum of work. He is, essentially, interested (and talented) in practical things, like his father. Long ago, I persuaded him that this talent, in combination with theory, would lead to professional success. He will make an excellent electrical engineer.

James, Andrew's brother, is failing at school. He is not disruptive. In fact, he is pleasant and co-operative with me, but over the years efforts by his mother to do extra reading and extra spelling practice have met with fierce resistance. James is happier dismantling a motor-bike engine. Now, I am faced with a long, hard haul to improve his reading, spelling and writing. Better that this had been done at a younger age and progress monitored weekly, so that failing pupils see themselves "catching up" and even equalling those they perceive as "clever". All is not lost though, however far behind your child becomes.

A PROGRAMME FOR IMPROVING ENGLISH

Reading is at the centre of progress in English. There are two aspects to this:

1. THE MECHANICS OF READING

Alan, aged ten, still cannot sound out certain letters, let alone combinations. His education corresponded with a period when phonics was totally abandoned in favour of "osmotic" learning. Reading, like any learning, is "built" by a combination of elements. If one element has been omitted, it makes it difficult for progress to occur.

These elements have to be learnt if reading is to be achieved:

(i) Letter sounds and shapes
(ii) Blend sounds and "shapes"
(iii) Word sounds, "shapes" and meanings

"Shapes" would include non phonetic blends (idio-syncrasies) like the "b" in thumb or the "h" in ghost.

With Alan, I go back to basics – the phonic alphabet, and showing Alan how to sound out "blends" (bl, br), etc. Within a few weeks his reading has improved dramatically, and with it so has his spelling. Everything is achieved by linking the abstract symbols to a picture ("a" for apple, "fl" for flower, etc).

2. INTEREST IN READING

A child must be interested in reading. Stories need to be imaginative, exciting and humorous as well as well-structured for reading attainment level. I buy Alan a series of books which provide a sentence or two per page printed beneath clear, colourful pictures. They have humour, adventure, and magic between the pages. For the first time in his life, Alan begins to be enthralled.

"He reads those books again and again," his mother tells me a month later.

Look carefully at the books you are selecting for your child. Is the reading level appropriate? Is the story exciting enough? (If you find it boring, your child certainly will. Also, some extraordinarily boring children's books have magnificent covers.)

WRITING

Many children, including good readers and spellers, dislike writing, in particular having to dream up creative efforts. Writing, in the league table of children's likes and dislikes at school, comes bottom, just after maths. Boys who are fast learners and read very little, underachieve astonishingly in this area. Faisal, aged nine, who was far ahead of his class in maths and could read well, struggled to write a few lines:

"He never reads books," said his mother. "I bring them home every week from the library, but he never reads them."

Todd was a boy who wrote even less for his school writing – one line on average. Yet in all other aspects of schoolwork he excelled – the school psychologist gave him an I.Q. of 140.

The answer is encouragement. Bilu's parents could accelerate his maths and English basics through basic exercises, but left it to me to advance his writing. He thrived under this type of regime:

"Just write about what you have done over the last week," I said. We discussed what could be put into the piece. He produced a page and a half of foolscap, occasionally stopping to ask me for a word to be spelt for him – and this was a boy pronounced unteachable by his teachers!

The remedy is to provide clear objectives, e.g. *this* story with *this* title, and also one-to-one "encouragement" (sitting next to him or her and giving a helping hand whenever necessary). From simple day-to-day diaries and reproductions of stories a child knows, can be developed the ability to create their own situations. Writing about videos and films they have seen is very productive. Vanessa was a girl who wrote nothing of value until she saw a Walt Disney film of Cinderella. The story she wrote was remarkable for an eight-year-old.

Writing helps to improve the stock of word meanings if you suggest "alternatives" to overused words (e.g. "nice" and "then" should be limited). It also gives an opportunity to point out where capitals and full stops should be placed and, as confidence grows, commas and speech marks.

This does not "come" all at once. It is a long process. Some children "learn" from reading books, but even for good writers several things should be pointed out:

(i) A sentence often needs to be "worked on" to convey the best effect.

(ii) There must be movement and humorous observation in a story, and a sense of the passing of time.

(iii) Conflict is the essential element for a good story (good against bad, man against the elements, etc).

(iv) Description needs to include colour, sounds, smells, textures, etc.

(v) Dialogue must reflect real life, but needs to be "spiced up" for story writing (otherwise dialogue would be of the "what bad weather we're having" and "pass the butter, please" variety. In general, people who talk in books are far more clever and witty than 99.99 per cent of ordinary people).

1. HANDWRITING
"Look at my writing," says Salma. "I don't think it's good enough. Do you?"

I think she is seeking reassurance, or perhaps is just fishing for praise. Her handwriting is excellent, probably better than mine. The difficulty is that presentation should at least be at a level that allows for easy reading. Average ideas in a well presented (good handwriting) form often score higher with teachers than good ideas presented through very scrappy handwriting. Unfortunately, some brilliant pupils' handwriting is terrible.

A word processor, of course, eliminates the variation in handwriting. It allows creative work to be judged relatively objectively.

Chapter Nine

PROBLEM SOLVING AND INVESTIGATIONS

Failure in problem solving at pre-eleven-years is often due to a failure to understand words or concepts. A slightly unusual way of presenting a problem can totally "throw" a child.

Sometimes, a problem can represent a totally different concept to one the child has learnt. Yesterday, Samantha, aged seven, was trying to solve:

10

8

"How many   more than   ," involves fairly complicated dissection and re-assembly to complete in her mind. Initially, she does not understand the concept of "more than" – "adding" is *combining* two or more numbers. "More than" is a comparison of two numbers. The link with adding and subtraction is easy to forge, but it needs separate practical work to build this on to memory.

In the second place, she is asked to visualise ten faces and eight umbrellas. With other difficulties this requires too many mental pictures to be carried in the mind at one time. A line of faces and a line of umbrellas should have been drawn for ease of comparison, and for meaning to be realised. After a little practice, Samantha raced away with the problems.

At a slightly higher level, words still cause problems:

"What does 'subtract' mean?" asked Debbie, aged nine. Then later, "What does 'total' mean?" "Increase" and "decrease" often defeat even good ten and eleven-year-olds (average fifteen-year-olds are also confused by the same terms – usually they do not know whether to use subtraction or division for decrease).

DISSECTING A PROBLEM

After word meanings have been explained, a child needs to learn how to dissect a problem, work out the individual sums/parts and then re-join the solutions to produce an overall solution.

Shopping problems illustrate the process. Salma is presently learning how to solve: "I have ten pounds. I buy one book, two dolls, and a toy car. How much change do I have?" She gets me to draw the items for buying:

£1.50   £2.30   95p

(Sometimes, she insists on doing the drawings herself.) Now, she adds up the money:

1.50		
2.30		
2.30		10.00
0.95	then takes	- 7.05
	from £10	
7.05		2.95 change

A few weeks ago this process was considered impossible to learn by Salma.

"It's too hard," she said.

I persuaded her: "Remember that two months ago you were in the yellow set, the bottom one at school. Now you've been moved up, and you're as good as anyone." She talks in terms of "clever" and "thick", as do many children (usually this rather stark and cruel grading of pupils comes from the parents, and other children).

Once Salma, like all children, has a clear vision of the overall process, has linked it into memory, and can recall the image easily, she is happy. Understanding and an increase of knowledge brings with it a sense of satisfaction and security. Learning, after all, is a mechanism for survival within a particular environment. If there are too many elements in the environment that are not understood, then insecurity develops with the failure, and even fear. This leads many children to "shut off" in the face of new learning, and particularly with problem solving.

TYPES OF PROBLEM SOLVING

The above is an example of the type of problem most widely found in problem solving, *convergent* problem solving, in which there is only one correct answer. *Divergent* problem solving involves a problem in which there are several answers to one problem. In science, you could ask, for example, how you could stop heat escaping from a house in the winter. However, this particular question is one much used in tests and exams, and thus can be revised for.

Much more akin to creativity is to ask a child a question that he or she is most unlikely to have heard before like, "Think of as many ways as you can that your headmaster can use to keep cool in his office in the hot summertime."

It is important to include even silly answers because sometimes these are the best solutions (how many children would think of "have his hair cut" because much heat is lost from the head area?). Divergent problem solving probes the extent of knowledge, but also probes the ability to develop creative links between widely separated groups of knowledge. Simply because of this wide divergence, links can sometimes seem wildly idiosyncratic, even childish (Einstein's illustration of his "Theory of Relativity" using trains is an example of idiosyncratic linking). It also encourages children not to overlook the obvious, a fact I have to stress to highly intelligent eighteen-year-olds, often utterly bemused by divergent problem solving in biology, and the lateral thinking required for solutions.

Problem solving consists of patterns and strategies that can be visualised, linked into memory and recalled when needed. A pattern that can be visualised includes the "find the change" problem, and the strategies involved in divergent problem solving can similarly be visualised, linked and recalled. This suggests that all types of learning occur in the same way. There is a high creative element in problem solving, the linking of concepts, patterns and strategies that are widely divergent – a struggle to create a new view of life, or indeed, something concrete that is entirely new.

PRE-SCHOOL PROBLEM SOLVING AND INVESTIGATIONS

At this age, there is much testing and trying of the environment. It is both physical and mental, developing in memory knowledge for survival in the home, garden, street, etc.

Your child *is* an investigator, he *is* a problem solver, but the patterns of knowledge that he builds up are not necessarily useful for school survival. He plays, but you as parent provide the environment. So, for part of the day at least, provide experiences that will make his transition to schoolwork that much easier.

Useful materials include water, sand, plasticine or play-doh, pots and pans and a good set of wooden bricks. However, simply providing these for free play is not enough – you also need to provide the stimulus for investigative and problem-solving thinking.

1. WATER
At the sink or in the bath, provide your child with things that float, things that sink, and plastic cups of various sizes. Show her how to pour water from cup to cup. To John, aged three, I would say:

"See how many float and how many sink," and leave him to it. When he was older I tried to develop with him a plasticine "boat". I was hopeless at it – the thing never floated. Some time later, after one particularly long water-play session, John announced:

"I've made the first plasticine ship."

I inspected it, carrying three marbles across the vast expanse of the kitchen sink.

"You've got to make it thin," he said, "or it sinks too low, and all the water comes in."

So *that* was how you did it! Not for the first time, a child had shown me how to do something.

2. SAND
A few kilos of sand in a cat litter tray provide much play value, and you can also show your child how to trace shapes, and later letters.

3. ALL THE SENSES
The creation of multi-sensory images is at the root of perfect learning and perfect recall. Although a child is using all his senses every day of his life, it is the early training of his *conscious* application of these senses to school related work (including problems) which is important.

Underneath a cloth I hid an apple, a brick, a toy car and a spoon.

"Feel underneath," I told Mark, aged four, "and try to imagine what you are feeling."

"The apple is easy," he said, "because I can smell it anyway, and it's got a stalk."

Games like this stimulate visualisation, as do making "hidden" sounds, or playing "blindfold tastes" (he closes his eyes, and tries to identify jam, lemon juice, etc. on a spoon). Later, this can be linked to visualising letters, words, spellings, ideas, problems, even strategies for investigations in school work. Your input as a parent is to make him aware of the value of internalised visualisation, and the creation of mental images and pictures.

4. GENERATING THINKING

Ultimately, the aim of investigative work and problem solving, is to get a child to "think for himself", to break away from a reliance on "rules". To have confidence in one's own reasoning, to discover for oneself, is a joy not to be missed. It involves an adventure into an insecure world, however. Experiences with high-flying university entrants have convinced me that great success can be achieved by working within learnt rules and strategies, but such students, when asked to think for themselves outside the range of such circular thinking, collapse into puddles on the ground.

Pre-school age and in early school life is the time to inculcate good habits of thinking by providing opportunities for a child to discover *some* things for himself. The benefit of discovery is in the strategies and attitudes learnt as well as in the stimulation of interest. In general, however, simply informing your child is more effective (and quicker), as long as the rules of mind-matching are adhered to.

5. INVESTIGATIONS TO TRY

(i)   Measuring in the house and garden.
(ii) Growing seedlings.
(iii) Looking at and talking about fruits and vegetables.
(iv) Trees in the environment.
(v)   Birds in the garden.
(vi) Animals at the zoo.
(vii) Seaside animals and plants.

(viii)Sounds.

(ix) Colours, light and dark: rainbow, spectrum, the sun, the moon.

(x) Pets (or a pet).

(xi) Looking in books at the variation in Life (using children's encyclopedias, etc.).

(xii) Materials: are they solid, liquid or gas?

(xiii)Looking at forces in everyday life: sport, toys, cars, aeroplanes.

(xiv) The seasons: looking at how things change over the year.

(xv) Using a weighing balance to compare weights.

(xvi) The history of the local area.

(xvii)Simple maps: of the local area, or to use on trips and holidays.

The above are only a small selection of possible investigations you can try before school, or to supplement school work. The importance of these, apart from the knowledge gained, is in the development of a way of thinking. Investigations with your child also need to start up separate trains of thought apart from the investigations themselves.

John, aged three, was growing mustard and cress seedlings:

"It grows slow," he said, rather surprising me.

"I think it's fast," I said, "because it's grown-up in a few days. It takes you much longer to grow up."

He thought for a minute. "Why does it take so long for me to grow up? Why can't I be big quick?" he asked.

There was no simple, straightforward answer to that, but, importantly, he was linking growth of plants to his own experience. Time and again, pre-school children do this, whereas teenagers are often limited by the task they are doing.

6. CREATIVE THINKING

In many books and in many people's minds, there are clear demarcation lines to be drawn between subjects like creativity and investigations, creativity and problem solving. This, in the light of how learning occurs, seems to be an artificial imposition. Children gain in knowledge and they can also link *internally* between groups of knowledge. So, an investigation has the elements of problem solving, but it is also creative, drawing together items of knowledge for consideration and use.

Creative thinking in a pre-schooler starts at a very young age indeed, and in particular through play. "Knowing" things extends the range of creative thinking, but you as a parent need to provide materials and an area in which to play.

Creative thinking can be stimulated through:

(i) Play with toys that can be used to explore real-life behaviour: house, figures of people, cars, buses, fire-engine, post-van, shop, zoo, farm, etc.

Marbles, building bricks and other building materials (e.g. Lego) are also used by a child in an imaginative way to represent real-life things (e.g. a marble as a man, a cuboid as a train).

Using such materials a child can reinforce what he learns in real-life, and also explore the limits of possible behaviour.

(ii) Dressing-up, acting out videos, TV programmes, etc. This also extends into pure imaginative (creative) play.

(iii) Painting, modelling, making collages, using plasticine and clay reflect both a desire to express and explore feelings, develop representations of real-life and even create new form.

The above activities, in concert with knowledge building, provide a platform from which school creativity can develop. Internalised linking of ideas along with the visualisation it creates is the essence of creativity. It has an overspill into education and life that is immeasurable.

Chapter Ten

MATHS EXERCISES TO DO WITH YOUR CHILD

NOUGHT TO TWO YEARS

These activities are mostly for ages one to two years.

1. COUNTING
(i) Many parents teach their children counting before they're two years old. Start by counting to three and reciting rhymes, for instance:

1, 2, 3
Have a cup of tea.

1, 2, 3
Mother caught a flea,
Put it in a tea-pot,
Made a cup of tea.
The flea jumped out,
Mother gave a shout,
In came Tommy with his
Shirt hanging out.

Add a little tune to increase enjoyment, and count the 1, 2, 3 on your fingers (or your child's fingers).

(ii) Count objects (1, 2, 3 plates, 1, 2, 3, dolls etc), steps when walking up and down stairs (1, 2, 3...1, 2, 3... 1, 2, 3 ...), fingers, etc.

2. PLAYING
Try not to be too intrusive into play – show something, and build on it.

(i) Get a set of bricks of all sorts of shapes and sizes. It should include different shapes: "square", "rectangle", "triangle", "parallelogram". Cubes and cuboids of various sizes, spheres, prisms, cylinders, pyramids are all very useful.
   Show them how to:
a. Build bridges.
b. Put cubes in order from the biggest to the smallest (using up to three cubes).

(ii) Plastic cups can be used for building, and for investigating *quantity* – of water in the bath, or sink.

TWO TO THREE YEARS

1. EXTENDING COUNTING
(i) Take the lead from your child, but five is a good number to aim for:
   Try this familiar rhyme on their fingers, or toes:
1 – this little piggy went to market

2 – this little piggy stayed at home
3 – this little piggy had roast beef
4 – this little piggy had none
5 – this little piggy went wee, wee, wee, wee...all the way home.

To the tune of ten green bottles, count:

"One big teddy sitting on the wall," etc up to five. Actually using teddies re-inforces the image (sit them on the table or settee alongside each other).

You can extend the counting in rhymes as is appropriate. However, you should be "slow but sure" adding two or three numbers at a time.

2. OTHER ACTIVITIES

(i)   Build towers as before. The towers will be much taller now. You can use plastic cups or wooden bricks.

(ii) Put cubes in order from the biggest to the smallest, using four or five objects now.

(iii) *Sorting*
Get your child to sort wooden bricks for *shape* (only two shapes in a pile of, say, six bricks at any one time) and for colour (two colours at first, with six bricks).

Other things which can be sorted include socks, toys, clothes, cutlery and dishes.

(iv) *Matching*
Get your child to match (pair) knives and forks, cups and scissors from a small, mixed pile.

THREE TO FIVE YEARS

1. COUNTING
Get your child to count the following:
(i) *Up to 5*
a. 0 0 0 0
b. 0 0
c. 0 0 0
d. 0 0 0 0 0
e. 0

(ii) *Up to 10*
a. 0 0 0 0 0 0 0
b. + + + + + +
c. 0 0 0 0 0 0 0 0 0
d. • • • • • • • • •
e. X X X X X X

2. COUNTING UP AND DOWN
Get your child to count *up* and *down* a number line, like this one. If your child is well-practised in this it will make adding and subtracting easier.

```
——— 10
——— 9
——— 8
——— 7
——— 6
——— 5
——— 4
——— 3
——— 2
——— 1
——— 0
```

3. SHAPES

(i) Draw shapes for your child: a square, a rectangle, a triangle and a circle. Ask them to name the shapes.

(ii) Ask your child to point out everyday objects which are square shapes, rectangle shapes, etc.

(iii) Draw shapes for your child and ask them to copy the shapes.

(iv) Get your child to recognise patterns of shapes. Draw a triangle, a square, a triangle, a square, a triangle...then ask them what shape should come next.

FIVE TO SEVEN YEARS

1. COUNTING

To avoid early troubles in maths, your child must be proficient at counting.

(i)   Practise counting up to 15 *and* back.

(ii) Do the following exercise with your child. Ask, "How many are left?"
a.   0 0 0 0 ~~0~~
b.   0 0 ~~0 0 0~~
c.   0 ~~0 0 0 0~~
d.   0 0 0 ~~0 0~~
e.   ~~0 0 0 0 0~~

   You can make this exercise more difficult (using more 0s) as your child becomes more competent.

2. ADDING

• ••
a.   1 + 2 =

•• •
b.   2 + 1 =

• •
c.   1 + 1 =

•• ••
d.   2 + 2 =

••• •
e.   3 + 1 =

3. USING THE NUMBER LINE FOR ADDING

(i) Show your child how to add on the number line by starting counting on the *next* number.

```
5 ─┬─
4 ─┼─
3 ─┼─
2 ─┼─
1 ─┼─
0 ─┴─
```

(ii) Try out the following sums using the number line:
a.   1 + 2 =
b.   2 + 2 =
c.   3 + 1 =
d.   1 + 1 =
e.   2 + 3 =

WELL DONE!

4. TAKING AWAY
(i) Ask your child, "How many left?" in the following sums. Use buttons or counters to illustrate them:

a.   3 - 1 =
    0 0 ө

b.   4 - 2 =
    0 0 ө-ө

c.   3 - 2 =
    0 ө-ө

(ii) Repeat sums by counting back on the number line, and then by using fingers.

All the above activities form a grounding in certain concepts (e.g. counting, addition, subtraction).
   You can develop all the above exercises as your child becomes more able:

 – extend the number line up to twenty, and practise adding to make a total of between ten and twenty, and then between twenty and thirty.

 – use the extended number line for subtracting large numbers.

The following exercises will also strengthen weaknesses where children often fail.

5. UNDERSTANDING SHARING
Ask your child to share sweets among two girls. (It's best to use real sweets if possible.)

a. 0 0 0 0
b. 0 0 0 0 0 0
c. 0 0 0 0 0 0 0 0
d. 0 0
e. 0 0 0 0 0 0 0 0 0 0

6. TIMES TABLES
As an introduction to the times table, ask your child how many twos there are in these?

a. 0 0 0 0
b. 0 0 0 0 0 0
c. 0 0 0 0 0 0 0 0
d. 0 0

7. MORE TIMES TABLES
a. $2 + 2 + 2 =$
b. $2 + 2 =$
c. $2 + 2 + 2 + 2 =$
d. $2 + 2 + 2$ is $3 \times 2 =$
e. $2 + 2 + 2 + 2 + 2$ is $5 \times 2 =$
    (1   2   3   4   5)

8. TIME ON THE CLOCK
What are the following times?

____ o'clock   ____ o'clock   ____ o'clock   ____ o'clock

9. COUNTING MONEY

a.　2p　1p　1p
b.　2p　2p　1p
c.　2p　1p　1p　1p
d.　2p　2p　2p　1p
e.　5p　2p　1p

10. CHANGE

Your child has 5p.

a.　Spend 1p:
　　5 - 1 =　　　　p change
b.　Spend 2p:
　　5 - 2 =　　　　p change
c.　Spend 3p:
　　5 - 3 =　　　　p change

SEVEN TO ELEVEN YEARS

1. TENS AND UNITS

Use paper strips, marked off, to ensure your child understands tens and units. Ask them questions such as these:

What numbers are these?

a.   **Tens Units**   b.   **Tens Units**

c.   **Tens Units**

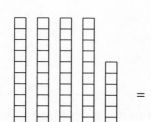

2. ADDING WITH TENS AND UNITS (CARRYING)

Show your child how adding with tens and units works, for instance:

  1 6   6   2 2

Try out these sums using paper tens and units:

a. 13 + 7 =   T U
                 1 3
              +   7
              _____

              _____

b. 18 + 9 =   T U
                 1 8
              +   9
              _____

              _____

c. 15 + 8 =   T U
                 1 5
              +   8
              _____

              _____

d. 16 + 6 =   T U
                 1 6
              +   6
              _____

              _____

Make up your own sums to use with paper tens and units.

3. TAKING AWAY USING TENS AND UNITS
Using paper strips shows how "borrowing" actually works.

a.

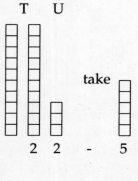

b.

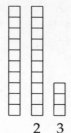 take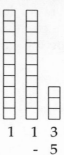

T U   T U

2 3   -   5   1 1 3
                  -   5

c. ^{1}2 ^{1}4   d. ^{2}3 ^{1}0

   -      7   -   6

_____   _____

_____   _____

4. FURTHER TIMES TABLES

Using the strips helps a child to understand what multiplication actually is:

1 x 5 = 5   (one lot of five)

5 x 5 = 25      (five lots of five)

5. DIVISION
Use the 2 x table for learning division. Make sure they realise the connection. Say, "How many twos in..." and try out the following sums on your child.

a. 2) 4
    ⊙⊙

b. 2) 6
    ⊙⊙⊙

c. 2) 8
    ⊙⊙⊙⊙

d. 2)12

e. 2)18   etc.

6. DIVISION WITH REMAINDERS

        1 r1
    2) 3   *one* 2, remainder 1
       ⊙ .

           r
a. 2) 5
    ⊙⊙ .

106

b. $\overline{2)\,7}\,^r$

c. $\overline{2)\,9}\,^r$

d. $\overline{2)11}\,^r$

Show them how to carry the remainder over:

a. $\dfrac{1\,5}{2)3\,{}^10}$

b. $\dfrac{1}{2)3\,{}^12}$

c. $\dfrac{1}{2)3\,{}^14}$

d. $\dfrac{1}{2)3\,{}^16}$

107

7. TELLING THE TIME

Ask them to say where the large hand (minute hand) is pointing *first*.

Quarter past

Quarter to

Half-past

Minutes past

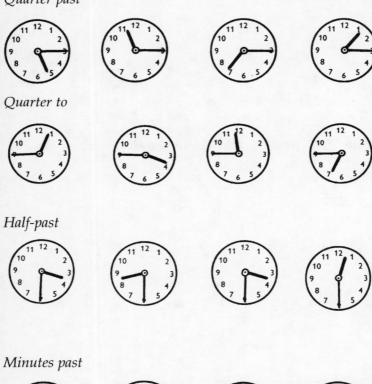

Minutes before

Your child also needs to know that time can be worked out in two ways: e.g. 20 to 11 is also 10.40. Practise with a clock with moveable hands.

ADDITIONAL PRACTICE

(i) Find these times past on the clock:
    0 past, 11 past, 18, past, 17 past, 4 past

(ii) Find these times to on the clock:
    4 to, 17 to, 24 to, 12 to, 8 to

(iii) Find these times:
    35 past, 45 past, 40 past, 53 past, 50 past

8. HUNDREDS, TENS AND UNITS: ADDING AND SUBTRACTING

a. 1 2 3   b. 2 4 6   c. 3 5 8
    + 3 7   + 2 5   +1 6 7
    _____   _____   _____

    _____   _____   _____

WELL DONE!

d. 7 2 4   e. 8 1 5   f. 7 2 3
    -1 1 5   -2 3 4   -1 3 5

9. MULTIPLYING

15   5   10
x2   is   x2 and x2

30   10   20

                   ↓

                   10
          +   20
                   30

a. 1 6   b. 1 7
    x 2   x 2

c. 1 8   d. 1 9
    x 2   x 2

110

d. 125
  x 2
  ———
  ———

e.   136
    x 2
    ———
    ———

f.   148
   x 2
   ———
   ———

10. FRACTIONS

(i) State the shaded portions

a.

b.

c.

(ii) How many halves in:

a. 1 whole   b. 2 whole   c. 3 whole   d. 1½

(iii) How many quarters in:

a.

one

b.

three

c.

1½

d.

2½

EQUIVALENT FRACTIONS

It is easier for your child to see if you show them a table.

½				½				halves
¼		¼		¼		¼		quarters
⅛	⅛	⅛	⅛	⅛	⅛	⅛	⅛	eighths

(i) How many quarters in a half?

(ii) How many eighths in:

     a.   ¼   b.   2/4   c.   ¾

(iii) Add:

a. ¼ + ¼ = /4 = /2   b. ¼ + ¼ + ¼ = /4

c. ⅛ + ⅛ = 2/8 = /4   d. ⅛ + ⅛ + ⅛ + ⅛ = 4/8 = /4 = /2

e. ¼ + ⅛ = 2/8 + ⅛ = /8   f. ¼ + 2/8 = /8 + 2/8 = /8 = /4

112

(iv)

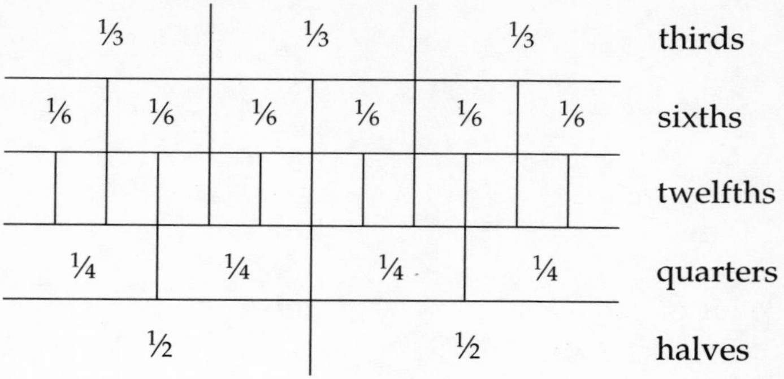

⅓		⅓		⅓		thirds
⅙	⅙	⅙	⅙	⅙	⅙	sixths
						twelfths
¼		¼		¼		¼	quarters
½			½			halves

a. $\frac{1}{3} + \frac{1}{2} = \frac{4}{12} + \frac{6}{12} = \frac{\ }{12} = \frac{\ }{6}$

b. $\frac{1}{4} + \frac{1}{3} = \frac{3}{12} + \frac{4}{12} = \frac{\ }{12}$

11. MEASUREMENT

a.   1 metre   =   cm

b.   ½ metre   =   cm

c.   ¼ metre   =   cm

d.   ¾ metre   =   cm

e.   2½ metres   =   cm

WELL DONE!

f.   1 Kg   =   g

g.   ½ Kg   =   g

h.   ¼ Kg   =   g

i.   ¾ Kg   =   g

j.   1 Litre   =   ml

k.   ½ Litre   =   ml

l.   ¼ Litre   =   ml

m.   ¾ Litre   =   ml

12. SHOPPING SUMS

(i)   I have £5. I buy these things:

   2 books at £1.20 each, and 3 packets of sweets at 45p
each. How much change do I have?

   a.   Total   1.20   b.   Change   £5.00
                      1.20   -
                      0.45
                      0.45   _____
                 +   0.45
                                              _____
                      _____

                      _____

114

(ii) I have £20. i buy 3 books at £1.50 each, 6 bars of chocolate at 45p each, and a toy at £7.50. How much change do I have?

13. DECIMALS

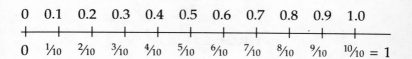

(i) Change to one decimal place:

a. $\frac{3}{10} =$ b. $\frac{3}{10} =$ c. $\frac{3}{10} =$ d. $\frac{3}{10} =$

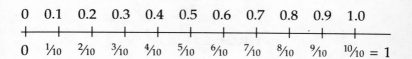

0 0.01 0.02 0.03 0.04 0.05 0.06 0.07 0.08 0.09 0.10 0.11 0.12 0.13 0.14

$\frac{1}{100}$ $\frac{2}{100}$ $\frac{3}{100}$ $\frac{4}{100}$ $\frac{5}{100}$ $\frac{6}{100}$ $\frac{7}{100}$ $\frac{8}{100}$ $\frac{9}{100}$ $\frac{10}{100}$ $\frac{11}{100}$ $\frac{12}{100}$ $\frac{13}{100}$ $\frac{14}{100}$

$\frac{1}{10}$

(ii) Change to two decimal places:

a. $\frac{3}{100}$ b. $\frac{7}{100}$ c. $\frac{11}{100}$ d. $\frac{14}{100}$

Chapter Eleven

ENGLISH EXERCISES TO DO WITH YOUR CHILD

PRE-SCHOOL

There are several areas which, if neglected pre-school, lead to failure in schoolwork. The words below need to be learnt over a period of years. They represent a basis of what a child should know before starting school.The meaning should be clear to your child, although they would not be expected to be able to read them.

1. NAMING WORDS

Objects in the home: table, chair, radio, TV, window, tools, computer, kettle, settee (sofa), curtains...etc.

Clothes: pyjamas, shorts, gloves (mittens), blouse, scarf, skirt, nightdress, jumper, cardigan, vest, shirt, trousers, tie...etc.

Food: milk, biscuits, cake, beefburger, bread, meat, egg, sandwich, jam, fruit (tomato, apple, banana, orange, grapes, pear, grapefruit, etc), vegetables (carrot, cabbage, onion, peas, potatoes, beans, etc)...etc.

Outside objects: garage, garden, yard, tree, leaf, bush, flower, plant, weed, ground (earth), path, road...etc.

Transport: car, bus, train, taxi, bicycle (bike), tricycle (trike), boat, ship, ambulance, fire engine, submarine...etc.

Parts of the body: eye, ear, mouth, hair, nose, lips, tongue, teeth, chin, eyebrow, neck, shoulder, arm, hand...etc.

The family: dad (daddy, father), mum (mummy, mother), son, daughter, aunt, cousin, grandma, grandpa, twins, niece, nephew, husband, wife...etc.

Animals: dog, cat, puppy, kitten, horse, cow, sheep, duck, goose, swan, bird, mouse, rat, fox, frog (tadpole), fly, bee, wasp, ladybird, mosquito, lion...etc.

Colours: red, yellow, green, blue, pink, purple, orange, black, white, grey, brown, etc.

Shapes: square, rectangle, triangle, circle, cube.

Jobs: doctor, shopkeeper, dentist, driver, factory worker, manager...etc.

2. DOING WORDS
Sit, walk, run, jump, hop, skip, read, write, colour, draw, paint, dance...etc.

You could ask your child to act out these words.

3. ASK YOUR CHILD
(i) To say the days of the week.

(ii) The times of the day when she has breakfast, lunch, tea, dinner, goes to bed, gets up in the morning. Show her the times on the clock.

(iii) About winter, summer, spring, autumn:

It is hot in _____ summer
It is cold in _____ winter
Leaves fall in _____ autumn
Leaves come back in _____ spring

(iv) The opposites to these words (speaking):
up (down), cold (hot), fat (thin), short (tall), big (small), sad (happy), on (off), dirty (clean), light (heavy), over (under) etc.

FIVE TO SEVEN YEARS

1. THE PHONIC ALPHABET
Test only five letters of the phonic alphabet at a time.

(i) Draw pictures for your child, or use an A-B-C book: "a" for apple, "b" for banana, etc.

(ii) Use solid letters, plasticine models, real-life objects, or repeated drawings. A small notebook with similar repeated drawings can "animate" the letters (move them about), and this helps to achieve focus and linkage into memory.

2. BUILDING WORDS
Using the phonic alphabet to build words, get your child

to repeat these words after you.

cat, dog, hat, bag, tap, dot, pen, bed, leg, pig, lip, gun, sun, cup, pin, tin.

You can sound out the individual letters: "p - i - g".

3. COMMON WORDS IN READING

The following words should be written separately and practised.

Short vowel (easy structure): a, and, in, is, it, of.

Other: he, I, to, was; that, the (the "th" sound needs to be emphasised).

EXERCISE FOR READY-TO-READS:

Write these words on card (without capitals) and draw a simple picture above.

(i)   it is a cat.

(ii)   *th*at is a dog.

(iii) he is a man.

(iv)   go to bed.

(v)   *th*e sun is up.

(vi)   get the gun.

(vii) I ran to Sam.

      I run to Sam.

(viii) on *th*e top is a dot.

(ix)   *th*e pig is big and fat.

(x)   it was hot in *th*e sun.

4. MORE WORDS COMMON IN READING

Short vowel (easy structure): as, at, but, for, had, him, his, not, on.

Other: all, be, are, have, one, so, we, said, with, they, you.

WELL DONE!

TWO AND THREE LETTER WORDS GROUPED ACCORDING TO THE SHORT VOWEL:

Group 1

at	man	bat	bad	bag	cam	bap
an	can	cat	cad	fag	jam	cap
	ban	fat	dad	gay	ham	gap
	fan	hat	fad	lag	ram	lap
	pan	mat	had	rag	Sam	map
	ran	pat	lad	tag		nap
	tan	rat	mad	wag		rap
		sat	sad	nag		tap

Group 2

off	not	pod	bog	cop
on	cot	cod	hog	mop
of	hot		dog	lop
	pot		log	top
	dot			hop
	not			
	tot			

Group 3

men	bet	bed	beg	hem
den	met	led	leg	
pen	pet			
ten	set			

Group 4

in	bin	bit	bid	big	him	hip
it	din	fit	did	dig	rim	pip
if	tin	hit	hid	fig	dim	lip
	fin	kit	kid	pig		sip
	gin	lit	lid	wig		tip
	pin	pit		gig		rip
	sin	sit				nip
	win					

Group 5

up	bun	but	bud	bug	gum	cup
	fun	cut	dud	dug	hum	pup
	gun	gut	mud	rug	mum	sup
	nun	hut	hug	rum		
	pun	nut	mug	tum		
	run	rut	tug	sum		
	sun					

These groups serve well later as spelling groups. However, your child will need to be reading first. Hearing a sound, finding the linked word and writing it down is more difficult then seeing the word and trying to find the sound link.

5. FURTHER READING PRACTICE
Use simple picture books, especially of fairy stories, with preferably no more than one short sentence per page beneath a picture. The above work has emphasised *structure*, but reading a story with your child will alert him to

the thrill of reading. One without the other can lead to failure, boredom and disinterest.

6. EARLY WRITING
Like early reading this stretches from the three to four age group through to starting school.

PRACTICE 1
Using a crayon or pencil get your child to practise drawing horizontal, vertical and oblique straight lines on large sheets of paper, then circular and wiggly lines. Later, your child can practise these lines and variations.

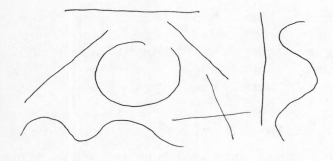

This may take several months if your child is still two, or a little over three. At this age it can also be introduced in creative drawing.

PRACTICE 2
Take one letter at a time. Get your child to copy it on paper, trace over it, trace it in a sand-tray, or handle a 'solid' letter. Easiest letters tend to be "o" and "c". The hardest include: "k", "y", "g", etc.

7. MORE FURTHER READING

Explain the magic "e". Ask your child to sound out:
bit*e* hat*e* gat*e* lat*e* hop*e*   hug*e*   rod*e*   rud*e*

How far you now take phonics depends on how quickly your child has built up a bank of words from pre-reading.

Many of those with reading difficulties have to be taken back to these initial stages, including being shown how to break up words and read in structurally meaning-ful chunks:

fin - ish - ed   star - ted
com - for - ta - ble   fan - tas - tic

Endings in reading cause relatively little difficulty. It is the middles of many words which do not fit into the basic phonics system. The following spelling section is a list of many of these words.

SEVEN TO NINE YEARS

1. SPELLING

Spelling practice usually begins around seven years of age.

(i) Begin by testing in Groups 1 - 5 previously, used for early reading.

(ii) The following are further groups for testing:
Sea	eat	leaf	
sing	ring	fling	king
head	bread	dead	

WELL DONE!

boat	soap	road		
when	why	who	where	what
cry	fly	try	shy	
happy	mummy	silly	daddy	

out	shout	cloud	about
how	down	clown	
lamb	climb	thumb	
hour	ghost	rhyme	

fight	sight	light	night	right
fright	bright	tonight		
know	knee	knife		
write	wrist	wrong		

Make your own lists to try with your child.

2. PUNCTUATION
Put capitals and full stops in the following:

On monday, my mum and dad took me to the sea-side at blackpool it was very hot we all had ice-creams and my baby sister dropped hers on the sand later we had a ride at the fair it was very fast when we got off my dad was sick my mum said it was because he is weak like all men at 7 o'clock we went home.

3. WRITING STORIES
If your child has great difficulty writing a story, starting it for her often gets the flow going. Use simple language.

Finish off this story:

On Saturday I woke up and found that I was a giant. I was so big that my feet reached right across the room, and

124

out of the open window.

    I went downstairs. My mum and sister screamed and ran out of the house. I sat down and had breakfast. it was ten bottles of milk, fifty fish fingers and sixteen loaves of bread. Then I went outside...

NINE TO ELEVEN YEARS

1. MORE ADVANCED SPELLING GROUPS

Use the groups below as a starting point for testing:

cure	sure	fury	plural	
your	court	pour	favour	harbour
picture	capture	fracture	mixture	temperature
try	cry	marry	empty	worry
tried	cried	married	emptied	worried

careful	helpful	cupful	awful	beautiful
battle	little	apple	middle	cycle
bang	bung	song	long	wrong
comic	picnic	traffic	Atlantic	Arctic
bandage	cabbage	savage		

bridge	hedge	ridge	ledge	budge
million	region	onion	religion	
division	television	passion		
kindness	goodness	happiness		
bought	fought	thought		

2. FURTHER PUNCTUATION

In the following passages, put in full stops, capitals, commas, speech marks, exclamation marks and question marks:

Passage 1

billy ducked down his mother followed holding on to the table top to retain balance they faced each other under the table then billy feinted a move forward his mother dived at nothing billy jumped up and ran round the table while his mother was still full stretch on the floor billy come back do you hear I said come back.

(*A Kestrel for a Knave*: Barry Hines, 1968)

Passage 2 (The following passage also needs grammar correction):

school diary

the day I fell off the tower of terror

by benny benson

when we went on the day trip to the fair last week I were showing off on the roller-coaster and fell off at the start and when it came round for the second time mr hutchins my headmaster said cor benny benson what you doing standing on the railway for and I said please sir I'm trying to catch this train ain't I and my candy-floss blew right in his face didn't it and miss spruggins my teacher sat on my ice lolly and got a wet bum she were not very pleased and said something about taking me up the big wheel and launching me into space what is rather sarcastic isn't it

(*Samson Superslug* and the *Dracula Hunt*: Ken Adams, 1993)

CONCLUSION

"Failure" is an unfriendly word. It suggests that our single sojourn through this world, our life, has been wasted. Yet, all of us fail greatly in our lives, particularly if we measure our success against what might have been. This book has been concerned with one small area of life, in which unfulfilled potential destines most of us to waste our talents disastrously – that of pre-school and early school life.

I have seen countless small children restored to full confidence and success by applying basic principles of learning. A non-reader of seven heading for the inevitable unemployment queue, is taught to read in two weeks by his father, and becomes an electrical engineer. A small girl suffering from an intense fear of maths, is shown how to divide, and goes to university to study medicine. A boy of ten, unable to write a coherent story, is shown the way and one year later wins a scholarship to a top English public school, and goes on to outstanding success. No-one wants a child to fail, especially when methods are to hand that overturn the seemingly inevitable.